JUMBLE®

CROSSWORDS

A New Twist on an Old Favorite

by David L. Hoyt

TRIUMPH
B O O K S
CHICAGO

This book is available at special discounts
for your group or organization.

For further information, contact:

Triumph Books LLC
814 North Franklin Street
Chicago, IL 60610
(800) 888-4741
(312) 337-1807 FAX

ISBN: 978-1-57243-347-2

Printed in the USA

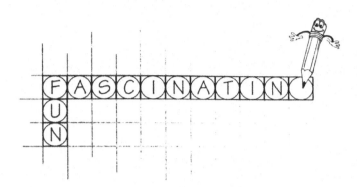

JUMBLE® CROSSWORDS

CONTENTS

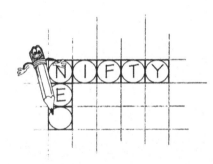

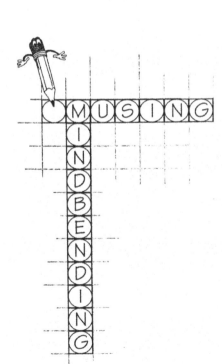

JUMBLE®
CROSSWORDS
CHAMPION PUZZLES

 #1

JUMBLE CROSSWORDS™

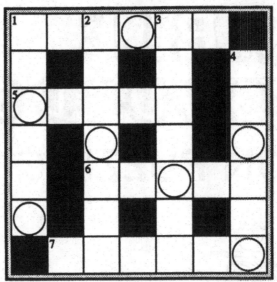

ACROSS

CLUE	ANSWER
1. To tell	FINMOR
5. May describe a *model*	LESAC
6. What ghosts do	AHNUT
7. A person in the middle	KBORRE

DOWN

CLUE	ANSWER
1. What a bee is	ISTCEN
2. It may classify a *bed*	HATEFER
3. A *retail* name	KCUBOER
4. A courting man	TRISOU

CLUE: A traveler

BONUS

How to play Complete the crossword puzzle by looking at the clues and unscrambling the answers. When the puzzle is complete, unscramble the circled letters to solve the BONUS.

JUMBLE CROSSWORDS™

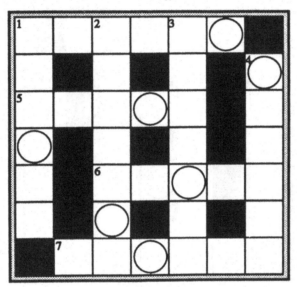

ACROSS

CLUE		ANSWER
1.	A blemish	MPPLEI
5.	A type of flower	CALLI
6.	You might have to dig it out	PUTMS
7.	Profession	RREEAC

DOWN

CLUE		ANSWER
1.	A type of star	SLAPUR
2.	A name	SAMLISE
3.	A type of speech	RUTCEEL
4.	Possibly *disposable*	PIDRAE

CLUE: Confident

BONUS

How to play Complete the crossword puzzle by looking at the clues and unscrambling the answers. When the puzzle is complete, unscramble the circled letters to solve the BONUS.

#3

JUMBLE CROSSWORDS™

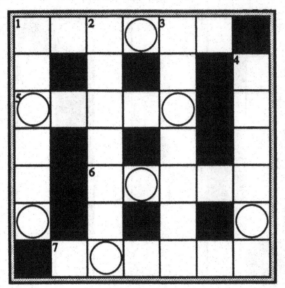

ACROSS

CLUE	ANSWER
1. This begins near an *end*	TINREW
5. *First, middle, last*	SMANE
6. Extend	HCRAE
7. A *CD* or *cassette* _____	YAPRLE

DOWN

CLUE	ANSWER
1. Sometimes *dead* or *alive*	DANWET
2. *One* is one	LAMRUNE
3. Extreme happiness	YATCSES
4. Fasten	HETTRE

CLUE: Settled comfortably

BONUS

How to play — Complete the crossword puzzle by looking at the clues and unscrambling the answers. When the puzzle is complete, unscramble the circled letters to solve the BONUS.

#4

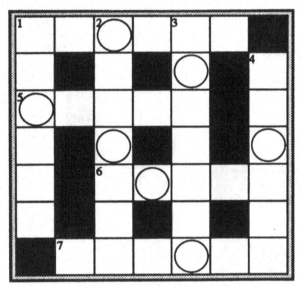

JUMBLE CROSSWORDS™

ACROSS

CLUE	ANSWER
1. Break off, separate	TEADCH
5. _____ away	HIDES
6. Works better if it is sharp	FINEK
7. Withdraw	PLEEAR

DOWN

CLUE	ANSWER
1. Term used with medicine	DAGSOE
2. Slow movement	KLECRIT
3. A pain reliever	OENIDEC
4. In a direct line	LLIAEN

CLUE: Yours may need to be *given*

BONUS

How to play Complete the crossword puzzle by looking at the clues and unscrambling the answers. When the puzzle is complete, unscramble the circled letters to solve the BONUS.

JUMBLE CROSSWORDS™

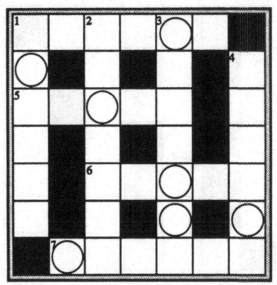

ACROSS

CLUE	ANSWER
1. Expire, run out, slip by	PASEEL
5. Second president	SAMDA
6. Nonsense	PITER
7. A body movement	GINCER

DOWN

CLUE	ANSWER
1. Found on teeth	MANLEE
2. This makes a change	PATADRE
3. A period of time	NOSSSIE
4. To make disappear	LEEDET

CLUE: You are *responsible* for yours

BONUS

How to play   Complete the crossword puzzle by looking at the clues and unscrambling the answers. When the puzzle is complete, unscramble the circled letters to solve the BONUS.

JUMBLE CROSSWORDS™

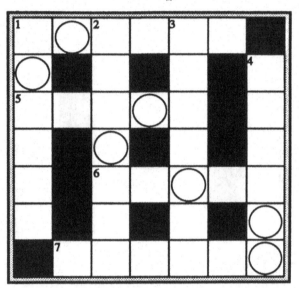

ACROSS

CLUE	ANSWER
1. An incentive to buy	TABEER
5. To make happen, push	CREOF
6. The opposite of credit	TIEDB
7. These glow	SEEBRM

DOWN

CLUE	ANSWER
1. A way to win a prize	FFELAR
2. A type of condition, state	MOODBER
3. Result of nervousness	BEEMTLR
4. A plant	STUCCA

CLUE: *Why*

BONUS

How to play

Complete the crossword puzzle by looking at the clues and unscrambling the answers. When the puzzle is complete, unscramble the circled letters to solve the BONUS.

JUMBLE CROSSWORDS™

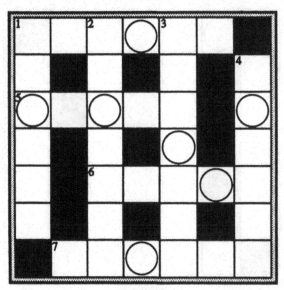

ACROSS

CLUE	ANSWER
1. Obscene	GRAVLU
5. A zodiac sign	BILAR
6. A woman's nickname	NNNAA
7. This can be a type of *pine*	TNYTKO

DOWN

CLUE	ANSWER
1. This is what *Spock* was	NCVALU
2. This borders Syria	NNOABLE
3. Contrary to	GINAATS
4. A reason to towel off	TASEWY

CLUE: A reason to take aim

BONUS

How to play — Complete the crossword puzzle by looking at the clues and unscrambling the answers. When the puzzle is complete, unscramble the circled letters to solve the BONUS.

8

PUZZLE #8

JUMBLE CROSSWORDS™

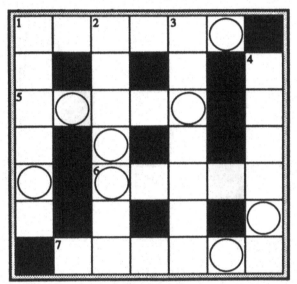

ACROSS

CLUE	ANSWER
1. This is something *given*	VADCIE
5. Gentle or dull	ADNLB
6. To bring together	TINUE
7. A rash might have done this	HITDEC

DOWN

CLUE	ANSWER
1. A city in New York State	BYNAAL
2. A type of bridge	VATCDUI
3. This is found in the ocean	HISCDOF
4. Part of a screw	DARHET

CLUE: You might want to *fill up* with this

BONUS

How to play — Complete the crossword puzzle by looking at the clues and unscrambling the answers. When the puzzle is complete, unscramble the circled letters to solve the BONUS.

9

PUZZLE #9

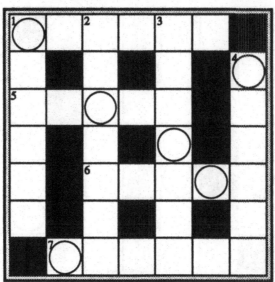

JUMBLE CROSSWORDS™

ACROSS

CLUE		ANSWER
1.	A unit based on years	DADCEE
5.	A type of poison	MEVNO
6.	To make a sound	TTERU
7.	Dull, uninteresting	GYDOTS

DOWN

CLUE		ANSWER
1.	A battle strategy	VEDIID
2.	To get an opinion	STUNLOC
3.	Reduced in level, rank	EEDDTOM
4.	A type of *red*	RRHEYC

CLUE: A type of *place*

BONUS

How to play Complete the crossword puzzle by looking at the clues and unscrambling the answers. When the puzzle is complete, unscramble the circled letters to solve the BONUS.

10

JUMBLE CROSSWORDS™

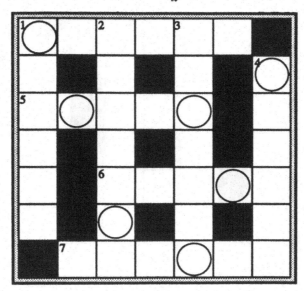

ACROSS

CLUE	ANSWER
1. Dirty	GYBBUR
5. A city in Japan	KAAOS
6. This is found in your mouth	LOMRA
7. A famous *Thomas*	OISNDE

DOWN

CLUE	ANSWER
1. A *Bush*	REGGOE
2. Having no *arms*	MARDENU
3. A famous foursome	STABLEE
4. Customer	NATROP

CLUE: You might require this to be *safe*

BONUS

How to play — Complete the crossword puzzle by looking at the clues and unscrambling the answers. When the puzzle is complete, unscramble the circled letters to solve the BONUS.

JUMBLE® CROSSWORDS™

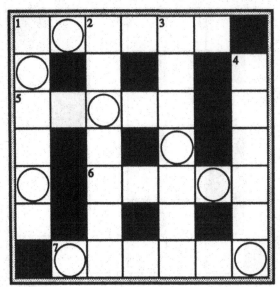

ACROSS

CLUE	ANSWER
1. This is something you *take*	R E S W H O
5. *Ant-_____*	T R A E E
6. A type of *nerve* or *cable*	T O P C I
7. To look for, to detect	S Y D E R C

DOWN

CLUE	ANSWER
1. A type of hammer	G E D S L E
2. An ending, result	U T O O C E M
3. Without order	T R A C I E R
4. This can describe a person	Y K O T S C

CLUE: This can brighten your day

BONUS

How to play   Complete the crossword puzzle by looking at the clues and unscrambling the answers. When the puzzle is complete, unscramble the circled letters to solve the BONUS.

JUMBLE® CROSSWORDS™

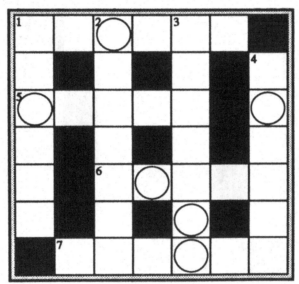

ACROSS

CLUE	ANSWER
1. Make aware	YITFON
5. You might monitor this	GASEU
6. Nonsense	MOKUH
7. This relates to wind	ZEREBE

DOWN

CLUE	ANSWER
1. An ill feeling	SAEUNA
2. Found in a classroom	HATRECE
3. This can appear on skin	KCEEFLR
4. To hinder, block	TYEIMS

CLUE: An opening, store or supply

BONUS

How to play   Complete the crossword puzzle by looking at the clues and unscrambling the answers. When the puzzle is complete, unscramble the circled letters to solve the BONUS.

#13

JUMBLE CROSSWORDS™

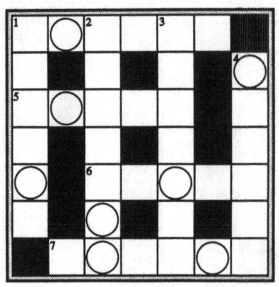

ACROSS

CLUE	ANSWER
1. Unfortunate, dreadful	GRAICT
5. _____ Asimov	ACAIS
6. The choice members	TILEE
7. A religious figure	TIPRES

DOWN

CLUE	ANSWER
1. This holds water	TTEIOL
2. This player is not paid	TRAAMUE
3. A hill	LINECIN
4. Strong	TTPNEO

CLUE: A type of shock

BONUS

How to play Complete the crossword puzzle by looking at the clues and unscrambling the answers. When the puzzle is complete, unscramble the circled letters to solve the BONUS.

JUMBLE CROSSWORDS™

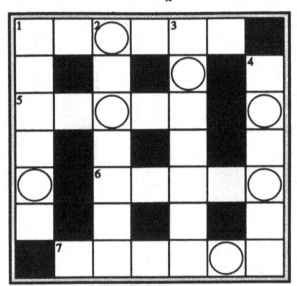

ACROSS

CLUE	ANSWER
1. This relates to heaviness	HEWGIT
5. Used like *cool*	TINFY
6. A thick skinned mammal	RONIH
7. This might make you laugh	DYOCEM

DOWN

CLUE	ANSWER
1. Cold, snowy	TRINYW
2. *The Towering* _____	FENINOR
3. Out of control	EAIRWYH
4. This might describe a *mess*	DOYLBO

CLUE: A vacation spot or "Maude" character

BONUS

How to play — Complete the crossword puzzle by looking at the clues and unscrambling the answers. When the puzzle is complete, unscramble the circled letters to solve the BONUS.

JUMBLE CROSSWORDS™

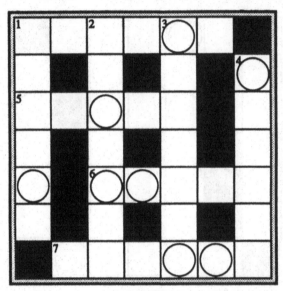

ACROSS

CLUE	ANSWER
1. A relative	SCUNIO
5. Country like	LURRA
6. Outspoken	CLAVO
7. Having outer metal layers	DATELP

DOWN

CLUE	ANSWER
1. A type of rule	FURCWE
2. Fall apart	VANRULE
3. Not legally permitted	TILILIC
4. Sent for delivery	ADIMEL

CLUE: Longer play or higher pay

BONUS

How to play — Complete the crossword puzzle by looking at the clues and unscrambling the answers. When the puzzle is complete, unscramble the circled letters to solve the BONUS.

JUMBLE CROSSWORDS™

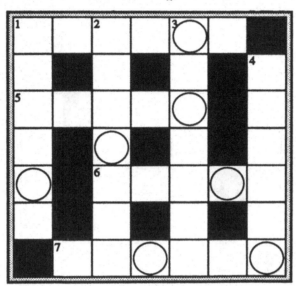

ACROSS

CLUE	ANSWER
1. Located in N. America	KAAASL
5. A fabric	STANI
6. A monetary unit	EPURE
7. A very handsome man	SAINDO

DOWN

CLUE	ANSWER
1. To take for granted	MESSUA
2. Changed	REDAETL
3. Important person	GINKNIP
4. Used for gripping, turning	SPREIL

CLUE: D.J., M.D., P.T. and M.N.

BONUS

How to play

Complete the crossword puzzle by looking at the clues and unscrambling the answers. When the puzzle is complete, unscramble the circled letters to solve the BONUS.

JUMBLE® CROSSWORDS™

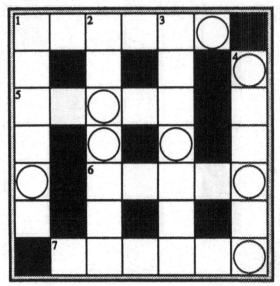

ACROSS

CLUE	ANSWER
1. What this is	ZLEPZU
5. Mean	TYNSA
6. A paperwork person	FLERI
7. Already over	DAYELP

DOWN

CLUE	ANSWER
1. This has two ends	PLINCE
2. Full of enjoyment	SLEZFTU
3. A type of faith	YYLLOAT
4. Regarded with reverence	SCARDE

CLUE: A great misfortune

BONUS

How to play Complete the crossword puzzle by looking at the clues and unscrambling the answers. When the puzzle is complete, unscramble the circled letters to solve the BONUS.

JUMBLE® CROSSWORDS™

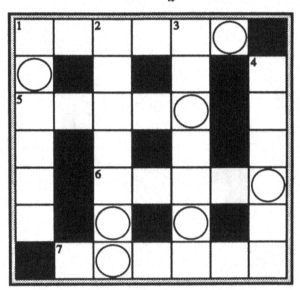

ACROSS

CLUE	ANSWER
1. A metal often used as trim	MECHOR
5. A type of used tire	PCEAR
6. This person is not smart	TIIOD
7. This can be measured	HHTGIE

DOWN

CLUE	ANSWER
1. Found on a computer screen	SCORRU
2. Lean back	LIRNEEC
3. Done with hands and arms	GINPPMO
4. A grouping	STTEEP

CLUE: A Roman god and a celestial body

BONUS

How to play — Complete the crossword puzzle by looking at the clues and unscrambling the answers. When the puzzle is complete, unscramble the circled letters to solve the BONUS.

PUZZLE #19

JUMBLE CROSSWORDS™

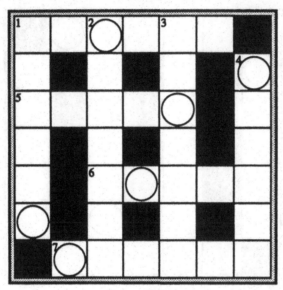

ACROSS

CLUE	ANSWER
1. Wrecked	DENURI
5. This can be performed	MAARD
6. A matter of dispute	SEUSI
7. Moved together	DREEDH

DOWN

CLUE	ANSWER
1. A rat is one	TENDRO
2. Dream, think	MAGNIIE
3. Slipped or passed by	SPALEDE
4. A way to cause death	DEEBHA

CLUE: These can be *good* or *bad*

BONUS

How to play — Complete the crossword puzzle by looking at the clues and unscrambling the answers. When the puzzle is complete, unscramble the circled letters to solve the BONUS.

20

PUZZLE

#20

JUMBLE® CROSSWORDS™

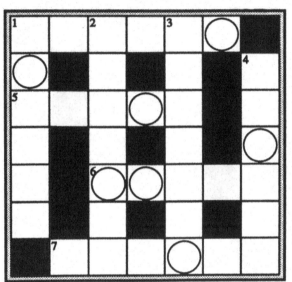

ACROSS

CLUE	ANSWER
1. Part of a car engine	TIPSNO
5. You could win this	WAADR
6. This can be a type of *cut*	APPER
7. A multi-*celled* environment	NIPRSO

DOWN

CLUE	ANSWER
1. This grows in the ground	TANPUE
2. A quick movement	PREMACS
3. A legendary king	DIPSUEO
4. To exceed; surpass	ROTUUN

CLUE: They are older than you

BONUS

How to play   Complete the crossword puzzle by looking at the clues and unscrambling the answers. When the puzzle is complete, unscramble the circled letters to solve the BONUS.

JUMBLE CROSSWORDS™

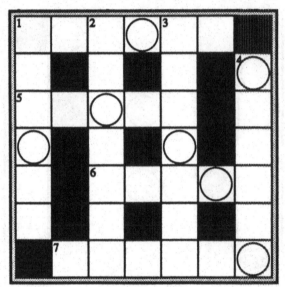

ACROSS

CLUE	ANSWER
1. A type of straight line	SPITRE
5. If you are this, you scratch	THYIC
6. You could *lose* yours	COVEI
7. A problem	SCIIRS

DOWN

CLUE	ANSWER
1. Dirty	SLIDOE
2. Bounce back	ROVERCE
3. What Newton studied	SSIHPYC
4. To locate data on computer	CACSES

CLUE: Of enduring interest

BONUS

How to play Complete the crossword puzzle by looking at the clues and unscrambling the answers. When the puzzle is complete, unscramble the circled letters to solve the BONUS.

JUMBLE CROSSWORDS™

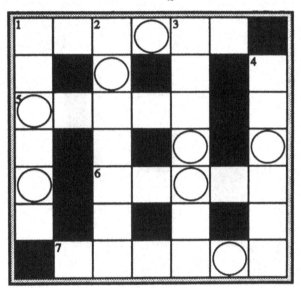

ACROSS

CLUE	ANSWER
1. Soak up	SBBOAR
5. This is something you *set*	CERIP
6. Cut, stab	FENIK
7. Light can be considered this	HITGRB

DOWN

CLUE	ANSWER
1. To become obvious	AAPPER
2. Sometimes found on a car	KITSREC
3. A type of movement	RLEEIGN
4. Missing	SABTEN

CLUE: A place with many *rooms*

BONUS

How to play — Complete the crossword puzzle by looking at the clues and unscrambling the answers. When the puzzle is complete, unscramble the circled letters to solve the BONUS.

PUZZLE #23

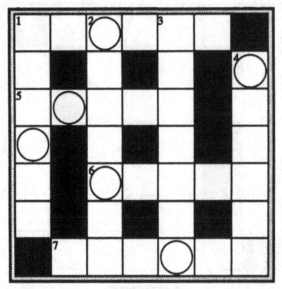

JUMBLE CROSSWORDS™

ACROSS

CLUE	ANSWER
1. Possible result of diving	HAPSSL
5. These can be *taken*	STOEN
6. Rule	GINRE
7. This can describe a dress	KINYLS

DOWN

CLUE	ANSWER
1. A governing body	TANEES
2. From or to the side	TRALLEA
3. A meeting or period	SSSOINE
4. Used primarily	YINMAL

CLUE: Average

BONUS

How to play Complete the crossword puzzle by looking at the clues and unscrambling the answers. When the puzzle is complete, unscramble the circled letters to solve the BONUS.

24

#24

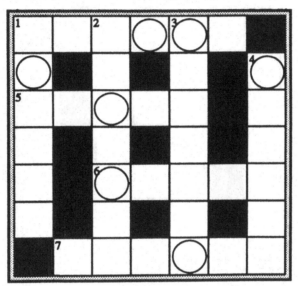

JUMBLE® CROSSWORDS™

ACROSS

CLUE	ANSWER
1. Your general condition	ATHHLE
5. Sometimes already seen	NRRUE
6. Stick to	DIBAE
7. A steep drop	GENLUP

DOWN

CLUE	ANSWER
1. A type of *crab*	TREHMI
2. A shipping process	LAMIIRA
3. Strain	SITNNEO
4. This might come in a block	EEESHC

CLUE: This has to do with the middle

BONUS

How to play — Complete the crossword puzzle by looking at the clues and unscrambling the answers. When the puzzle is complete, unscramble the circled letters to solve the BONUS.

JUMBLE CROSSWORDS™

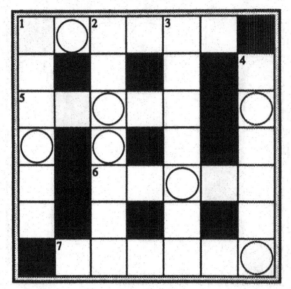

ACROSS

CLUE	ANSWER
1. A fictional *PI*	GAMMNU
5. Plan, organize, carry out	GESTA
6. Beginning	STOEN
7. Playful behavior	LRFOIC

DOWN

CLUE	ANSWER
1. To have been off target	SEDIMS
2. Alluring charm	LAGRUMO
3. A fork is one	STUNILE
4. A northern *circle*	TRACCI

CLUE: This can be used when speaking

BONUS

How to play   Complete the crossword puzzle by looking at the clues and unscrambling the answers. When the puzzle is complete, unscramble the circled letters to solve the BONUS.

JUMBLE CROSSWORDS™

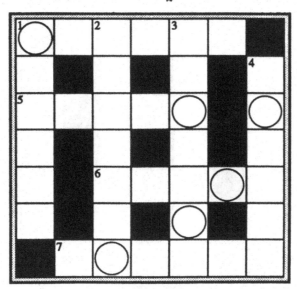

ACROSS

CLUE	ANSWER
1. Clever in practical matters	DREHSW
5. A runner might be one	ERRAC
6. _____ Asimov	ASCAI
7. Sometimes a likeness	TTUESA

DOWN

CLUE	ANSWER
1. Used like road	SETRET
2. A type of written record	PIREECT
3. This can be *issued*	RRAATNW
4. To make one's way by force	SLUCME

CLUE: Second largest, sixth farthest

BONUS

How to play Complete the crossword puzzle by looking at the clues and unscrambling the answers. When the puzzle is complete, unscramble the circled letters to solve the BONUS.

PUZZLE #27

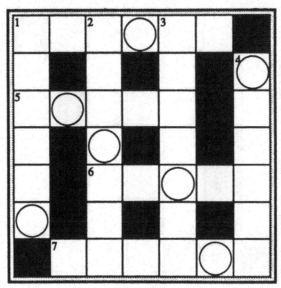

JUMBLE CROSSWORDS™

ACROSS

CLUE

1. A track or channel
5. Like an engine
6. Sometimes the boss
7. Achieve

ANSWER

VORGEO
TROOM
WENRO
TTAANI

DOWN

CLUE

1. A zodiac symbol
2. A type of station
3. This is often made of wood
4. A cell found in the body

ANSWER

IIMENG
STOPTUO
RAVEDNA
NNROEU

CLUE: Yours can be *given*

BONUS

How to play — Complete the crossword puzzle by looking at the clues and unscrambling the answers. When the puzzle is complete, unscramble the circled letters to solve the BONUS.

#28

JUMBLE CROSSWORDS™

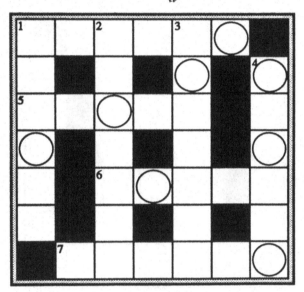

ACROSS

CLUE	ANSWER
1. You might *lose* if you do this	S O Z O E N
5. A woman's name	R A M A I
6. This relates to emotions	Y O D O M
7. For male and female	X N U E S I

DOWN

CLUE	ANSWER
1. A carpet _____	P M A S E L
2. Used to make a boat move	R A M N A O S
3. Full of fervor	S L E Z A U O
4. Found in the neck	R A X L Y N

CLUE: An astronaut can be considered one

BONUS

How to play Complete the crossword puzzle by looking at the clues and unscrambling the answers. When the puzzle is complete, unscramble the circled letters to solve the BONUS.

JUMBLE CROSSWORDS™

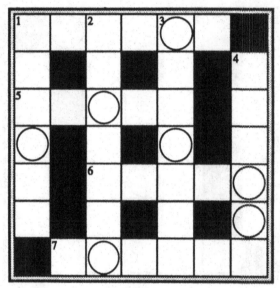

ACROSS

CLUE	ANSWER
1. *Instant* is a type of this	PAYLER
5. Usually considered *up*	HONTR
6. A body of water	CANEO
7. You must file to get one	TTENPA

DOWN

CLUE	ANSWER
1. A car or house can be one	TANREL
2. Character	SPRENOA
3. A boxer is one	HETLTAE
4. This has a shell	NAPETU

CLUE: Redford was one in a movie

BONUS

How to play — Complete the crossword puzzle by looking at the clues and unscrambling the answers. When the puzzle is complete, unscramble the circled letters to solve the BONUS.

PUZZLE #30

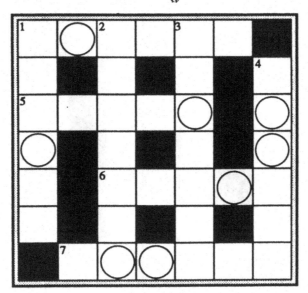

JUMBLE CROSSWORDS™

ACROSS

CLUE	ANSWER
1. Close, in the vicinity	BRANYE
5. These are found in water	SWEVA
6. This is always a female	CEEIN
7. Entangled	SDEMHE

DOWN

CLUE	ANSWER
1. A U.S. city	KENRWA
2. This can be a *payment*	CAAEDVN
3. Ask eagerly	EEESCHB
4. Show up, be there	DANTET

CLUE: You can find *tape* in one

BONUS

How to play Complete the crossword puzzle by looking at the clues and unscrambling the answers. When the puzzle is complete, unscramble the circled letters to solve the BONUS.

#31

JUMBLE CROSSWORDS™

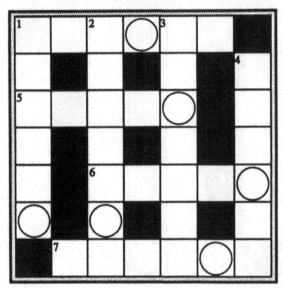

ACROSS

CLUE		ANSWER
1.	Usually done after a trip	CKNUAP
5.	A type of *headache*	UNSSI
6.	You turn into this over time	DTALU
7.	This covers sheep	ELEFEC

DOWN

CLUE		ANSWER
1.	Not secure	FANSUE
2.	This game has paddles	PLABLIN
3.	You can wear this	SOTMCEU
4.	A type of fight	LABTET

CLUE: A type of home

BONUS

How to play Complete the crossword puzzle by looking at the clues and unscrambling the answers. When the puzzle is complete, unscramble the circled letters to solve the BONUS.

32

PUZZLE #32

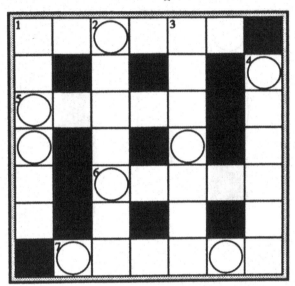

JUMBLE CROSSWORDS™

ACROSS

CLUE	ANSWER
1. A temple of the Far East	DAGOPA
5. _____ feelings	NIREN
6. A safe place	VNHEA
7. Boring, dull	GYTDOS

DOWN

CLUE	ANSWER
1. This is always a man	EPRCIN
2. This is often loud	TONHUSG
3. From a source	DDEEVIR
4. Vogue	TENYRD

CLUE: "An Elvis" can be a type of this

BONUS

How to play — Complete the crossword puzzle by looking at the clues and unscrambling the answers. When the puzzle is complete, unscramble the circled letters to solve the BONUS.

JUMBLE CROSSWORDS™

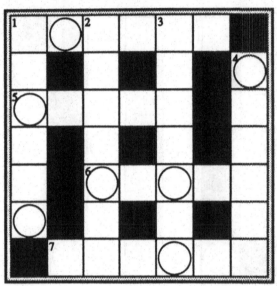

ACROSS

CLUE	ANSWER
1. A bad golfer	FEDRUF
5. This can be set to make noise	GRAEP
6. A typewriter type	TILEE
7. This can describe weather	MYSTOR

DOWN

CLUE	ANSWER
1. Leave	TRAPED
2. Created by the imagination	GINFTEM
3. Before	RAILREE
4. An acting *Irons*	MYJEER

CLUE: Known for being the largest

BONUS

How to play — Complete the crossword puzzle by looking at the clues and unscrambling the answers. When the puzzle is complete, unscramble the circled letters to solve the BONUS.

#34

JUMBLE CROSSWORDS™

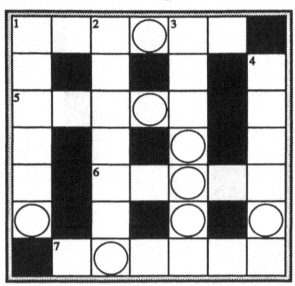

ACROSS

CLUE	ANSWER
1. To keep quiet	FYCIAP
5. A popular '70s sign	CEEPA
6. A woman's name	ALLIE
7. A riddle	GINMAE

DOWN

CLUE	ANSWER
1. _____ out, or _____ in	EPPPDO
2. A famous *Charlie*	HALNIPC
3. Running away	EFEGNIL
4. A song or a Hyundai	TANAOS

CLUE: An event that may have serious consequences

BONUS

How to play — Complete the croseword puzzle by looking at the clues and unscrambling the answers. When the puzzle is complete, unscramble the circled letters to solve the BONUS.

JUMBLE CROSSWORDS™

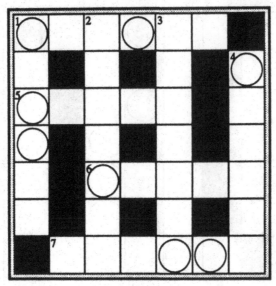

ACROSS

CLUE	ANSWER
1. Part of the eye	TANIER
5. Serious or solemn	BROSE
6. A famous *layer*	ZNEOO
7. A Texas city	SODAES

DOWN

CLUE	ANSWER
1. A country	SIRUAS
2. A type of newspaper	DITLOBA
3. You can feel this way	VENURSO
4. A place to see a movie	MINEAC

CLUE: These are handpowered

BONUS

How to play — Complete the crossword puzzle by looking at the clues and unscrambling the answers. When the puzzle is complete, unscramble the circled letters to solve the BONUS.

PUZZLE

#36

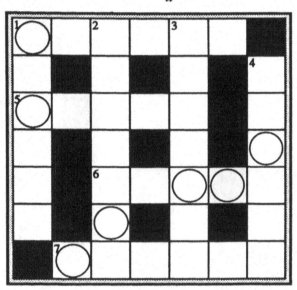

JUMBLE CROSSWORDS™

ACROSS

CLUE	ANSWER
1. Not much rhymes with this	GANERO
5. An FM receiver	RUNET
6. To cut with a knife	SILEC
7. _____ figure	HATREF

DOWN

CLUE	ANSWER
1. Everything you're wearing	TIOTUF
2. A reason to be forgetful	SIMEANA
3. This adds color to a meal	HINGRAS
4. Narrow, elongated	RAELNI

CLUE: Written words can be this

BONUS

How to play — Complete the crossword puzzle by looking at the clues and unscrambling the answers. When the puzzle is complete, unscramble the circled letters to solve the BONUS.

PUZZLE #37

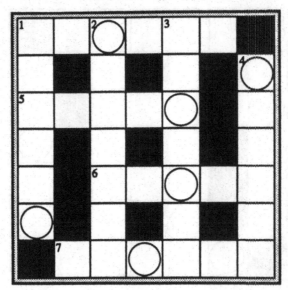

JUMBLE CROSSWORDS™

ACROSS

CLUE	ANSWER
1. To take away	KEEVOR
5. A type of warning	ISNRE
6. Fat	SEEOB
7. State of affairs	SSTTAU

DOWN

CLUE	ANSWER
1. Appropriate for the country	CURIST
2. A New England state	TORMENV
3. Nicest	STNDEIK
4. A break	SRSEEC

CLUE: A naturally dark place

BONUS

How to play Complete the crossword puzzle by looking at the clues and unscrambling the answers. When the puzzle is complete, unscramble the circled letters to solve the BONUS.

JUMBLE CROSSWORDS™

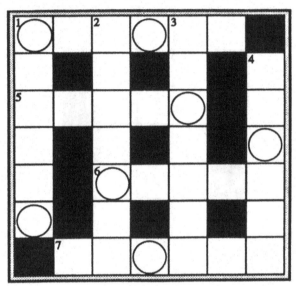

ACROSS

CLUE	ANSWER
1. A type of drawing	FLERFA
5. A view	STAVI
6. Public perception	GAMEI
7. To contaminate	TENICF

DOWN

CLUE	ANSWER
1. To go back to an old way	RVTREE
2. A _____ statement	HISFANO
3. A reason to fix a pipe	GAAELKE
4. To give emphasis to	CANTEC

CLUE: If this is *bad*, you might be late

BONUS

How to play — Complete the croseword puzzle by looking at the clues and unscrambling the answers. When the puzzle is complete, unscramble the circled letters to solve the BONUS.

PUZZLE

#39

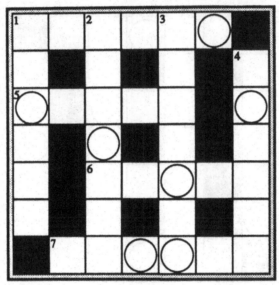

JUMBLE CROSSWORDS™

ACROSS

CLUE	ANSWER
1. This relates to sound	M E L U V O
5. A European river	N I R H E
6. To bring together	F I Y N U
7. Packed tightly	G D E W D E

DOWN

CLUE	ANSWER
1. Against	S V R E S U
2. Freedom from demands	S I L E R E U
3. A gathering	G E M T E N I
4. To have followed commands	Y D E O E B

CLUE: A family of actors (L.B., B.B and J.B.)

BONUS

How to play Complete the crossword puzzle by looking at the clues and unscrambling the answers. When the puzzle is complete, unscramble the circled letters to solve the BONUS.

40

JUMBLE CROSSWORDS™

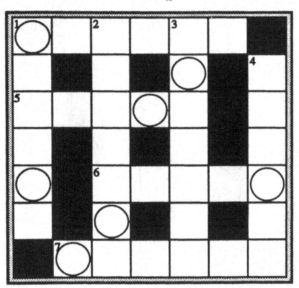

ACROSS

CLUE

1. To increase in size
5. Sometimes a type of *room*
6. Incompetent
7. _____ a needle

ANSWER

XDEANP
WELOB
PETNI
TADREH

DOWN

CLUE

1. Found on the face
2. To make publicly known
3. A Beatles *Man*
4. For all to see, read

ANSWER

YILDEE
IPBHSLU
WHENORE
STEPDO

CLUE: A film about Michael Dorsey as Dorothy Michaels

BONUS

How to play Complete the crossword puzzle by looking at the clues and unscrambling the answers. When the puzzle is complete, unscramble the circled letters to solve the BONUS.

JUMBLE® CROSSWORDS™

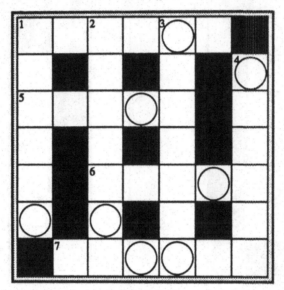

ACROSS

CLUE	ANSWER
1. A New York river	SUHNOD
5. Iron can become this	TYURS
6. Unfasten	PNINU
7. A valuable _____	NSOSLE

DOWN

CLUE	ANSWER
1. An exclamation of joy	HHRRUA
2. An argument, quarrel	STUPDIE
3. A legendary *Mount*	YSPMULO
4. You need a *ball* to fire this	NOCNAN

CLUE: Sean Connery is this

BONUS

How to play — Complete the crossword puzzle by looking at the clues and unscrambling the answers. When the puzzle is complete, unscramble the circled letters to solve the BONUS.

PUZZLE

#42

JUMBLE CROSSWORDS™

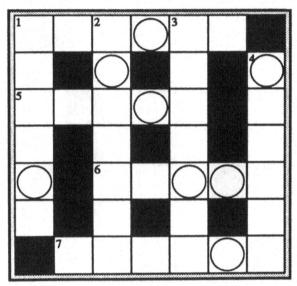

ACROSS

CLUE	ANSWER
1. Sudden or unexpected	BUTPRA
5. A type of weapon	FIREL
6. A sense	LEMSL
7. Around the longest	TEDLSO

DOWN

CLUE	ANSWER
1. The above clues direction	SRSAOC
2. To decline acceptance	RALUESF
3. To come before	CEPREED
4. A type of house	TECLAH

CLUE: You may be this now

BONUS

How to play — Complete the crossword puzzle by looking at the clues and unscrambling the answers. When the puzzle is complete, unscramble the circled letters to solve the BONUS.

JUMBLE CROSSWORDS™

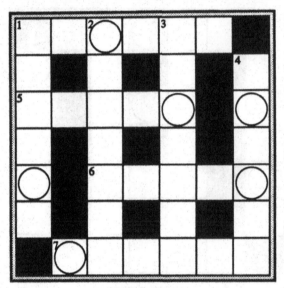

ACROSS

CLUE	ANSWER
1. _____ out	RFIUGE
5. The *Boston Garden* is one	AARNE
6. A language	NITLA
7. The main course	EEERTN

DOWN

CLUE	ANSWER
1. A European country	ENCFAR
2. An imaginary disruptor	LEMNIRG
3. You can cook in this	TRRSEOA
4. A game of _____	CCAENH

CLUE: You can make one, or carry some

BONUS

How to play   Complete the crossword puzzle by looking at the clues and unscrambling the answers. When the puzzle is complete, unscramble the circled letters to solve the BONUS.

#44

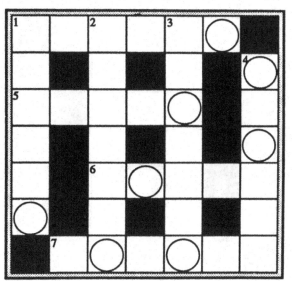

JUMBLE® CROSSWORDS™

ACROSS

CLUE	ANSWER
1. Rich and full-bodied	TORSUB
5. A place to get your hair cut	NLAOS
6. These can be *good* or *bad*	SIEBV
7. A place to find a plane	GANRAH

DOWN

CLUE	ANSWER
1. Hurried	DURHES
2. A South American country	LIBIAVO
3. Used to hold back water	GASNABD
4. Used to detect things	SSRENO

CLUE: This can come before *up*, *water* or *tall*

BONUS

How to play — Complete the crossword puzzle by looking at the clues and unscrambling the answers. When the puzzle is complete, unscramble the circled letters to solve the BONUS.

JUMBLE CROSSWORDS™

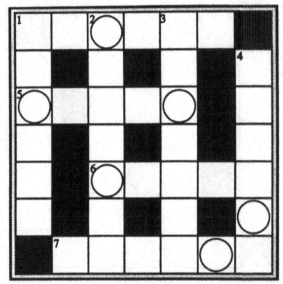

ACROSS

CLUE	ANSWER
1. A method of self-defense	TARAKE
5. A slight push	GEDNU
6. One of a printed series	SISEU
7. To make different	GNAHEC

DOWN

CLUE	ANSWER
1. A state and a rock group	SNSAAK
2. A shade	DIDESHR
3. This can be *committed*	SOTERNA
4. To blame without proof	GELALE

CLUE: A root used in food and drink preparation

BONUS

How to play Complete the crossword puzzle by looking at the clues and unscrambling the answers. When the puzzle is complete, unscramble the circled letters to solve the BONUS.

#46

JUMBLE CROSSWORDS™

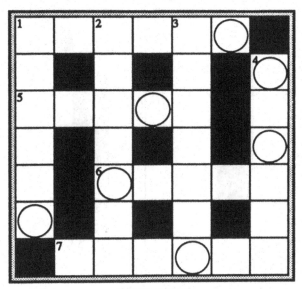

ACROSS

CLUE | **ANSWER**

1. Between small and large — MIDMUE
5. Part of a step — RESRI
6. Fictional helpers — ESLEV
7. A Soviet leader — NALITS

DOWN

CLUE | **ANSWER**

1. An acting *Rob* — WORMRO
2. Lineage — TENCEDS
3. To solve a mystery — LAVEURN
4. Picked — CONSHE

CLUE: You might have to look down to see this word

BONUS

How to play — Complete the crossword puzzle by looking at the clues and unscrambling the answers. When the puzzle is complete, unscramble the circled letters to solve the BONUS.

JUMBLE CROSSWORDS™

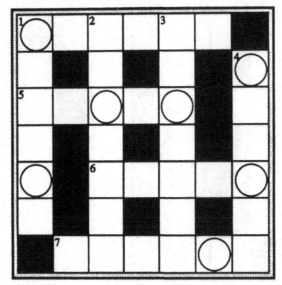

ACROSS

CLUE	ANSWER
1. An American Indian tribe	KAHWOM
5. Small	MORCI
6. A type of *switch*	GILTH
7. This usually comes in a box	YACNOR

DOWN

CLUE	ANSWER
1. A computer's capacity	YOREMM
2. A speaker's nightmare	HEELRKC
3. _____ accused	RYNGOLW
4. Buckle, attach	SFENTA

CLUE: A type of *zone* or *level*

BONUS

How to play Complete the crossword puzzle by looking at the clues and unscrambling the answers. When the puzzle is complete, unscramble the circled letters to solve the BONUS.

PUZZLE

#48

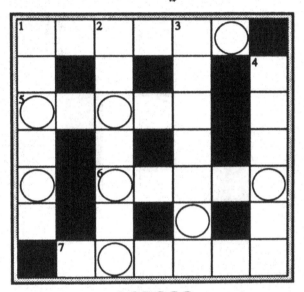

JUMBLE CROSSWORDS™

ACROSS

CLUE	ANSWER
1. On every occasion	YALSWA
5. To press into regular folds	PCMRI
6. A type of turn	SIWTT
7. A riddle or puzzling person	GAMINE

DOWN

CLUE	ANSWER
1. A Carroll O'Conner role	HIRCAE
2. _____ down	NETWITR
3. Useless talking	PAYNIPG
4. A writing *Christie*	TAGAAH

CLUE: This was *basic* to Michael and Sharon

BONUS

How to play Complete the crossword puzzle by looking at the clues and unscrambling the answers. When the puzzle is complete, unscramble the circled letters to solve the BONUS.

JUMBLE CROSSWORDS™

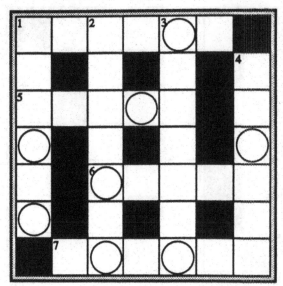

ACROSS

CLUE	ANSWER
1. This can be pulled from a hat	TRIBAB
5. Firm, strict	RETNS
6. Relating to the inside	RINNE
7. The _____ one	NOSEHC

DOWN

CLUE	ANSWER
1. A vacation place	STRERO
2. A type of flaw	SHIBMLE
3. Baseball increments	NNNSGII
4. One millionth of a meter	CORNMI

CLUE: Well-known, of great importance

BONUS

How to play   Complete the crossword puzzle by looking at the clues and unscrambling the answers. When the puzzle is complete, unscramble the circled letters to solve the BONUS.

PUZZLE

#50

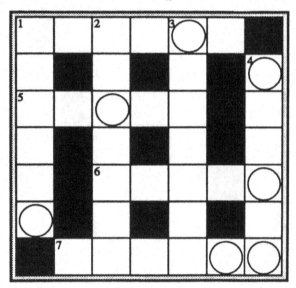

JUMBLE CROSSWORDS™

ACROSS

CLUE	ANSWER
1. An uninterrupted series	KTSARE
5. _____ thin	PRAEP
6. To make more exciting	VINLE
7. To send out troops	YOPLED

DOWN

CLUE	ANSWER
1. A type of *tank*	SPECIT
2. To drive back	SLUREEP
3. The end of a journey	VAIRALR
4. The chief part or point	MANYIL

CLUE: Guests can be considered this

BONUS

How to play Complete the crossword puzzle by looking at the clues and unscrambling the answers. When the puzzle is complete, unscramble the circled letters to solve the BONUS.

JUMBLE CROSSWORDS™

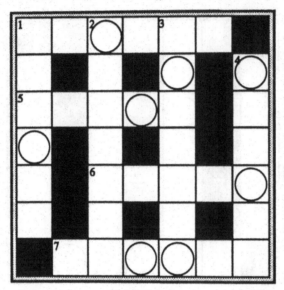

ACROSS

CLUE	ANSWER
1. Worn or run-down	BYBAHS
5. Home to a few *Dolphins*	IIMMA
6. A saying	GAADE
7. To send forth forcefully	HANLCU

DOWN

CLUE	ANSWER
1. Test, try out	PALMES
2. Home to Birmingham	BLAAAAM
3. Another name for England	TIBRINA
4. You can *give* one	SHECEP

CLUE: C.K.'s other name

BONUS

How to play Complete the crossword puzzle by looking at the clues and unscrambling the answers. When the puzzle is complete, unscramble the circled letters to solve the BONUS.

JUMBLE CROSSWORDS™

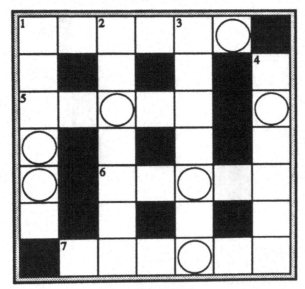

ACROSS

CLUE

1. Choose
5. Cat's have *nine* of these
6. _____ *spot*
7. A type of injury

ANSWER

CEETSL
ELVIS
DIBNL
ANIERH

DOWN

CLUE

1. A drinking establishment
2. Beyond likable
3. A chair might have one
4. A "Speed" star's name

ANSWER

NOLASO
BLAVOLE
HISCNOU
DANRAS

CLUE: A show of approval

BONUS

How to play

Complete the crossword puzzle by looking at the clues and unscrambling the answers. When the puzzle is complete, unscramble the circled letters to solve the BONUS.

PUZZLE #53

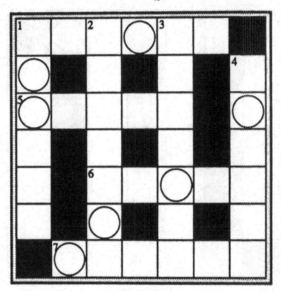

ACROSS

CLUE	ANSWER
1. An illusion	FADCEA
5. To escape capture	DELUE
6. A reference book	STAAL
7. One that sells	DENROV

DOWN

CLUE	ANSWER
1. A role played by a "Chevy"	CHELTF
2. Bravery	RAGEUCO
3. To have fought it out	DDELULE
4. Slang for mouth	SKIERS

CLUE: A group of *people* from the '70s

BONUS

How to play — Complete the crossword puzzle by looking at the clues and unscrambling the answers. When the puzzle is complete, unscramble the circled letters to solve the BONUS.

JUMBLE CROSSWORDS™

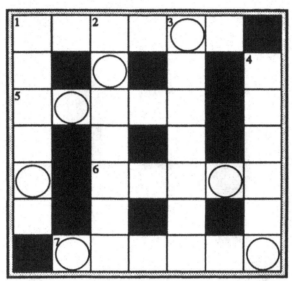

ACROSS

CLUE   **ANSWER**

1. Do again   TAPEER
5. A game played by two   SHECS
6. To take apart   GUNIR
7. This relates to the past   YAGCLE

DOWN

CLUE   **ANSWER**

1. Total _____   RALCEL
2. Assume   MUSEERP
3. A European country   TISRAAU
4. In a self-satisfied way   GUYLSM

CLUE: A famous *first's* first name

BONUS

How to play   Complete the crossword puzzle by looking at the clues and unscrambling the answers. When the puzzle is complete, unscramble the circled letters to solve the BONUS.

JUMBLE CROSSWORDS™

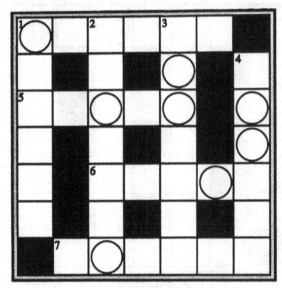

ACROSS

CLUE	ANSWER
1. Floating	FIDRAT
5. Really good	SPREU
6. A spoken language	HIISR
7. Testify or bear witness	TTTAES

DOWN

CLUE	ANSWER
1. Give out a task	GINSAS
2. Duplicate	PRENIRT
3. Pardon, understand	OFGRVEI
4. A final outcome	HUPTSO

CLUE: This can be a small book

BONUS

How to play — Complete the crossword puzzle by looking at the clues and unscrambling the answers. When the puzzle is complete, unscramble the circled letters to solve the BONUS.

PUZZLE

#56

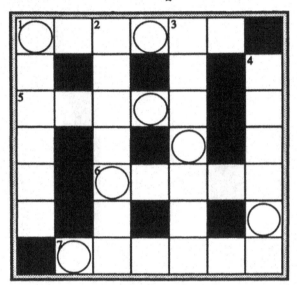

JUMBLE CROSSWORDS™

ACROSS

CLUE		ANSWER
1.	Flashing	BETORS
5.	A type of home	OLOIG
6.	Spanish for *father*	DAPER
7.	Your last cab	SEHARE

DOWN

CLUE		ANSWER
1.	Reiner's 'This is _____ Tap"	NISPLA
2.	A type of resumption	RPELESA
3.	Bigger	DABORRE
4.	Plot	SEEHCM

CLUE: Found in a bathroom; or a *W.B.* movie from 1975

BONUS

How to play

Complete the crossword puzzle by looking at the clues and unscrambling the answers. When the puzzle is complete, unscramble the circled letters to solve the BONUS.

JUMBLE CROSSWORDS™

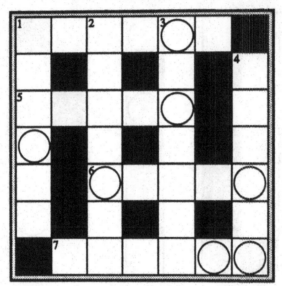

ACROSS

CLUE	ANSWER
1. A fee, cost, price	GRECAH
5. Bother	TEPUS
6. An animal sound	GINEH
7. _____ with	RCKENO

DOWN

CLUE	ANSWER
1. Reason to board a ship	SECURI
2. A period of being away	NABEECS
3. A British gateway	WKCITAG
4. A type of snake	YONHTP

CLUE: Void, zero or insignificant

BONUS

How to play Complete the crossword puzzle by looking at the clues and unscrambling the answers. When the puzzle is complete, unscramble the circled letters to solve the BONUS.

#58

JUMBLE CROSSWORDS™

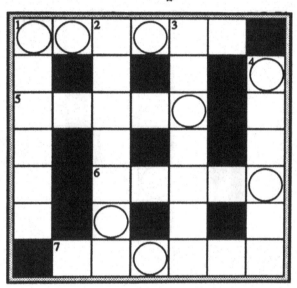

ACROSS

CLUE

1. Ostentatious
5. Known for its stripes
6. 'Lucy's' friend and neighbor
7. _____ weather

ANSWER

AYLFHS
AZBRE
LHEET
MSTYRO

DOWN

CLUE

1. To fail after a good start
2. Surrounding
3. A flower or woman's name
4. Rough, lacking order

ANSWER

ZELZIF
BIMTNAE
HHREEAT
WYLOLO

CLUE: More common the farther north or south you go

BONUS

How to play Complete the crossword puzzle by looking at the clues and unscrambling the answers. When the puzzle is complete, unscramble the circled letters to solve the BONUS.

JUMBLE CROSSWORDS™

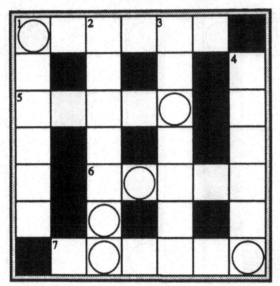

ACROSS

CLUE	ANSWER
1. _____ system	MCRETI
5. Nervous	STEEN
6. Remains	SNRIU
7. Reparation for a loss	SMANDE

DOWN

CLUE	ANSWER
1. Mom	HETRMO
2. Something you can *throw*	ARNTTMU
3. A European peninsula	BRIEIAN
4. An emergency	SSIIRC

CLUE: *Mona* hangs here

BONUS

How to play Complete the crossword puzzle by looking at the clues and unscrambling the answers. When the puzzle is complete, unscramble the circled letters to solve the BONUS.

JUMBLE CROSSWORDS™

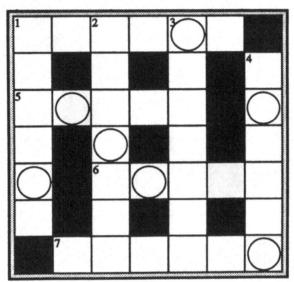

ACROSS

CLUE	ANSWER
1. A fix or cure	DEEYMR
5. _____ back	GYGIP
6. A memory can *strike* this	RCDHO
7. A type of phrase	GONALS

DOWN

CLUE	ANSWER
1. A "Jurassic Park" creature	RROPAT
2. Mysterious	GLACIAM
3. Dawn 'til dusk	GOYLNAD
4. A carried load	EBNDRU

CLUE: This performer's name might escape you

BONUS

How to play — Complete the crossword puzzle by looking at the clues and unscrambling the answers. When the puzzle is complete, unscramble the circled letters to solve the BONUS.

JUMBLE® CROSSWORDS™

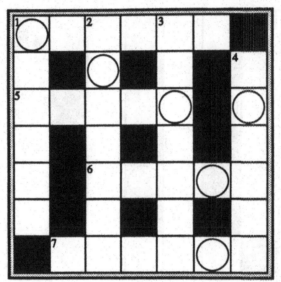

ACROSS

CLUE	ANSWER
1. _____ *academy*	CLOPIE
5. Part of the human body	ORTOS
6. They are known to laugh	NAYEH
7. A newspaper position	TRODIE

DOWN

CLUE	ANSWER
1. Short, small	ETTEIP
2. Pitched suddenly	DURLHCE
3. Calmest	STELOCO
4. A sweet treat	ERICAL

CLUE: A reason to get the scissors

BONUS

How to play · Complete the crossword puzzle by looking at the clues and unscrambling the answers. When the puzzle is complete, unscramble the circled letters to solve the BONUS.

JUMBLE CROSSWORDS™

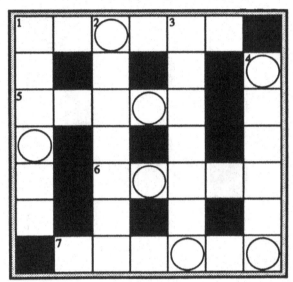

ACROSS

CLUE	ANSWER
1. Mr.	RETSIM
5. Stories	SLATE
6. Found in water or marsh	DERSE
7. Part of a corn plant	EELNRK

DOWN

CLUE	ANSWER
1. Reason	VITMOE
2. Indulge	GERSULP
3. Buddhism, Szechwan etc.	TANRESE
4. A tool used by some artists	SICHLE

CLUE: Permission

BONUS

How to play — Complete the crossword puzzle by looking at the clues and unscramble the answers. When the puzzle is complete, unscramble the circled letters to solve the BONUS.

#63

JUMBLE CROSSWORDS™

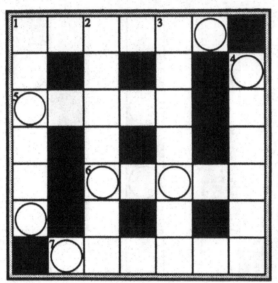

ACROSS

CLUE	ANSWER
1. Change	MERFOR
5. Punishment, beating	SCILK
6. Used like customers	SSREU
7. Light-hearted	HETLIB

DOWN

CLUE	ANSWER
1. _____ up or down	DRLOLE
2. True	CLAAUTF
3. This is earned	REPCEST
4. A woman's name	ISESJE

CLUE: The answer is this

BONUS

How to play Complete the crossword puzzle by looking at the clues and unscrambling the answers. When the puzzle is complete, unscramble the circled letters to solve the BONUS.

#64

JUMBLE CROSSWORDS™

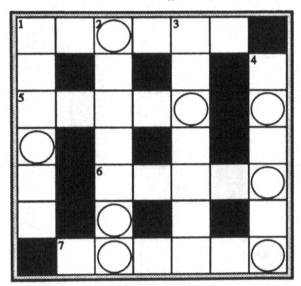

ACROSS

CLUE	ANSWER
1. A European capital	GURPAE
5. Burdened	NDLAE
6. A stopwatch is one	TIERM
7. A,B,C,D,F	DARSEG

DOWN

CLUE	ANSWER
1. _____ *holder*	YPCOIL
2. You might fear this person	ROTADIU
3. Identity unknown	UDENMAN
4. A type of group	HUSROC

CLUE: *George's* last or *Ford's* first

BONUS

How to play — Complete the crossword puzzle by looking at the clues and unscrambling the answers. When the puzzle is complete, unscramble the circled letters to solve the BONUS.

JUMBLE CROSSWORDS™

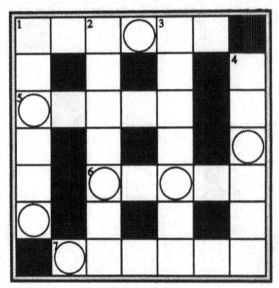

ACROSS

CLUE	ANSWER
1. A *Tom Hanks* movie	HAPLSS
5. A heart is one	GRANO
6. A European nobleman	NOCTU
7. A look	LEAGCN

DOWN

CLUE	ANSWER
1. This absorbs liquids	EOPGNS
2. Expected	GLACOLI
3. Possible result of clear day	SNNRUUB
4. _____ *Beach*	REMLYT

CLUE: Strength

BONUS

How to play — Complete the crossword puzzle by looking at the clues and unscrambling the answers. When the puzzle is complete, unscramble the circled letters to solve the BONUS.

PUZZLE

#66

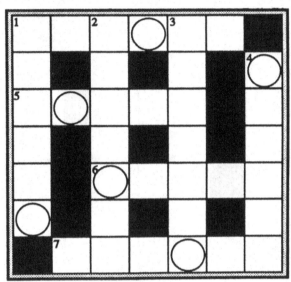

JUMBLE CROSSWORDS™

ACROSS

CLUE	ANSWER
1. One of the seven	PUREEO
5. Lessened	SDAEE
6. A king can be one	LRRUE
7. A type of gasoline	DDEEAL

DOWN

CLUE	ANSWER
1. XI	NEEELV
2. Put aside	VEEERRS
3. Sold	PDDDEEL
4. Shaken suddenly	RAJRDE

CLUE: A country, river or athlete

BONUS

How to play Complete the crossword puzzle by looking at the clues and unscrambling the answers. When the puzzle is complete, unscramble the circled letters to solve the BONUS.

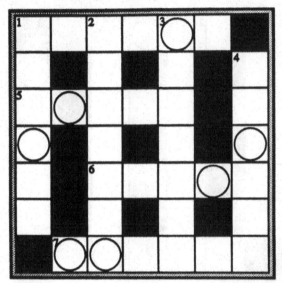

JUMBLE® CROSSWORDS™

ACROSS

CLUE		ANSWER
1. Quickly		POSTRE
5. Field of competition		RAAEN
6. Combination		NNIOU
7. A burden		GITHEW

DOWN

CLUE		ANSWER
1. Topped out		KAPEED
2. Carry out, accomplish		XEETUCE
3. Swapping		DINRAGT
4. A type of hat		NETNOB

CLUE: A+B+C can equal one

BONUS

How to play — Complete the crossword puzzle by looking at the clues and unscrambling the answers. When the puzzle is complete, unscramble the circled letters to solve the BONUS.

JUMBLE® CROSSWORDS™

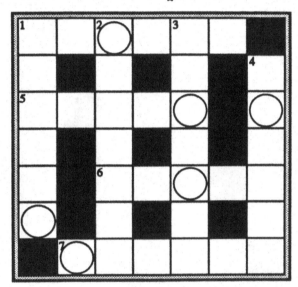

ACROSS

CLUE

1. Sound made by walking
5. You get this over time
6. _____ "G"
7. Member of rodent family

ANSWER

HQSSIU
DELRO
ADETR
REPHOG

DOWN

CLUE

1. Untidy
2. To be subjected to
3. Draw tight or taut
4. Think or speculate

ANSWER

POLPSY
RUNGEDO
CHESTRT
NERDOW

CLUE: Bacteria helps create this

BONUS

How to play
Complete the crossword puzzle by looking at the clues and unscrambling the answers. When the puzzle is complete, unscramble the circled letters to solve the BONUS.

#69

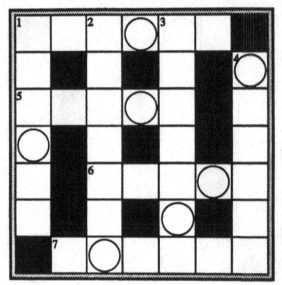

JUMBLE® CROSSWORDS™

ACROSS

CLUE	ANSWER
1. Part of New York City	NOPUTW
5. Used like factory	TANLP
6. Delicate	LIFAR
7. Spoken with ease	TENULF

DOWN

CLUE	ANSWER
1. Found behind *home*	REPIMU
2. Sad	RATFLUE
3. This relates to electricity	GATETAW
4. This can travel through air	BETLUL

CLUE: This *point* changes with altitude

BONUS

How to play — Complete the crossword puzzle by looking at the clues and unscrambling the answers. When the puzzle is complete, unscramble the circled letters to solve the BONUS.

JUMBLE CROSSWORDS™

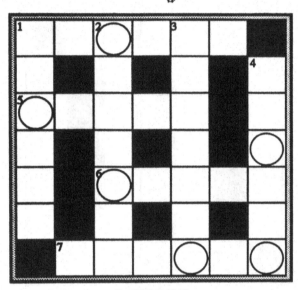

ACROSS

CLUE	ANSWER
1. Dust may cause one	ZENESE
5. A comparison	OTIAR
6. These can be trimmed	SLINA
7. A mark of reproach	GAMITS

DOWN

CLUE	ANSWER
1. This is full of *scenes*	TIPSRC
2. No longer around	NIXTETC
3. Moving quickly	NIMOZOG
4. A fictional "Brady"	SAMRAH

CLUE: A *James* that played a "Jim"

BONUS

How to play Complete the crossword puzzle by looking at the clues and unscrambling the answers. When the puzzle is complete, unscramble the circled letters to solve the BONUS.

JUMBLE CROSSWORDS™

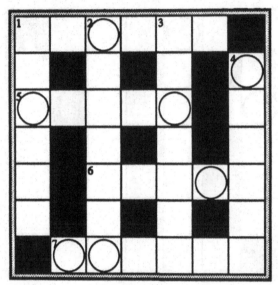

ACROSS

CLUE	ANSWER
1. A gentle breeze	PYHEZR
5. A fictional "Morgenstern"	DAROH
6. Containing charged atoms	CIINO
7. Ranked among the top	DEEEDS

DOWN

CLUE	ANSWER
1. Found in Switzerland	CHIZUR
2. Give	PORDIVE
3. Desired, wanted	EEDYNRA
4. Copied or tracked	TEDCAR

CLUE: A way to get from one point to another using your feet

BONUS

How to play Complete the crossword puzzle by looking at the clues and unscrambling the answers. When the puzzle is complete, unscramble the circled letters to solve the BONUS.

PUZZLE

#72

JUMBLE CROSSWORDS™

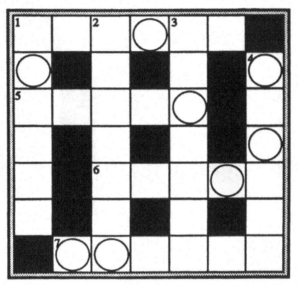

ACROSS

CLUE	ANSWER
1. Famous for its canals	NEVCIE
5. Sooner or _____	TRALE
6. Animallike	TURBE
7. A group of six	TTXEES

DOWN

CLUE	ANSWER
1. A logical spot to find a river	LAVYLE
2. Worth looking at	BATELON
3. A chain of theaters	IICCRUT
4. Smartest	STEWSI

CLUE: This is always a woman

BONUS ○○○○○○○○

How to play — Complete the crossword puzzle by looking at the clues and unscrambling the answers. When the puzzle is complete, unscramble the circled letters to solve the BONUS.

73

JUMBLE® CROSSWORDS™

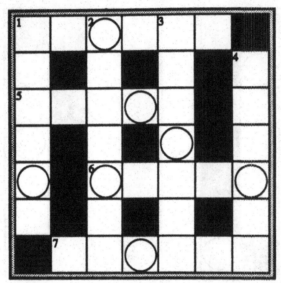

ACROSS

CLUE	ANSWER
1. Shriek	MASREC
5. _____ up	FILST
6. Gravy is considered this	CASEU
7. A blemish	HOTCLB

DOWN

CLUE	ANSWER
1. Combine, interweave	SEPCLI
2. Decline	SLAFURE
3. Attack	SATLUSA
4. 'Stalin's' first name	HOJPES

CLUE: You might find one on a table

BONUS

How to play — Complete the crossword puzzle by looking at the clues and unscrambling the answers. When the puzzle is complete, unscramble the circled letters to solve the BONUS.

JUMBLE CROSSWORDS™

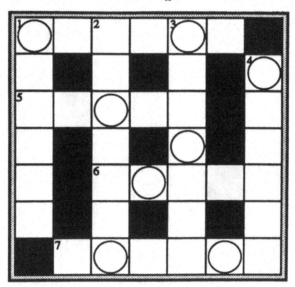

ACROSS

CLUE

1. A black eye
5. Contribution of ideas
6. To speak
7. _____ butter

ANSWER

HSIREN
TUPIN
RATEO
NAPTUE

DOWN

CLUE

1. Change
2. Burst inward
3. To go aboard a train
4. Choice, prime

ANSWER

TISHCW
PODLEIM
TANIRNE
TELSCE

CLUE: This can be *high, low* or *intense*

BONUS

How to play Complete the crossword puzzle by looking at the clues and unscrambling the answers. When the puzzle is complete, unscramble the circled letters to solve the BONUS.

JUMBLE CROSSWORDS™

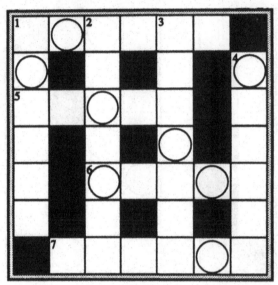

ACROSS

CLUE	ANSWER
1. Bite gently	BINLEB
5. A 1942 Disney film	IBBMA
6. Burned by a bad deal	GUSTN
7. Strangest	STEDOD

DOWN

CLUE	ANSWER
1. No person	NYDOOB
2. Confused	MEDSUEB
3. A type of *time*	RULISEE
4. A distressing situation	HITGLP

CLUE: H.S., M.S., B.S., L.S. and M.S. (fictional)

BONUS

How to play   Complete the crossword puzzle by looking at the clues and unscrambling the answers. When the puzzle is complete, unscramble the circled letters to solve the BONUS.

JUMBLE CROSSWORDS™

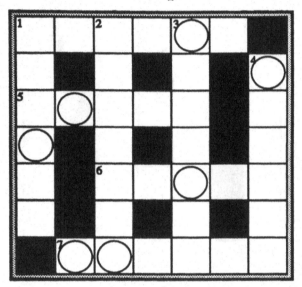

ACROSS

CLUE	ANSWER
1. A support	LAPLIR
5. Respond	TARCE
6. A four-legged animal	NEYHA
7. A fenced in area	SPRONI

DOWN

CLUE	ANSWER
1. Stationary	REDKAP
2. This comes from animals	HATREEL
3. A performer	STARSEC
4. Ancestry or descent	STINRA

CLUE: You might find one at the end of a wire

BONUS

How to play — Complete the crossword puzzle by looking at the clues and unscrambling the answers. When the puzzle is complete, unscramble the circled letters to solve the BONUS.

PUZZLE #77

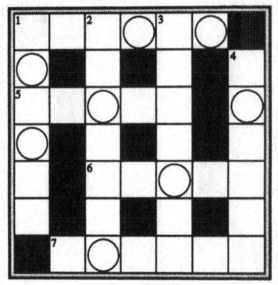

JUMBLE CROSSWORDS™

ACROSS

CLUE	ANSWER
1. Overlook	G I T L S H
5. Invalidate	L A N N U
6. Tracks	S L A R I
7. A musical term	G I D A A O

DOWN

CLUE	ANSWER
1. Disgraced	S H E D A M
2. Refrained from noticing	I R D E O N G
3. _____ hand	N I L P E H G
4. Complete failure	C O F S A I

CLUE: A beginning that feels like an ending

BONUS

How to play   Complete the crossword puzzle by looking at the clues and unscrambling the answers. When the puzzle is complete, unscramble the circled letters to solve the BONUS.

78

#78

JUMBLE® CROSSWORDS™

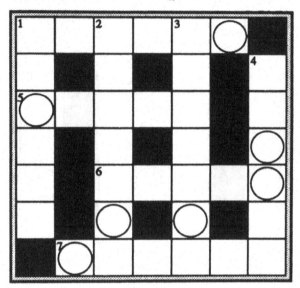

ACROSS

CLUE

1. This *justice* is fitting
5. King _____ XIV, XV or XVI
6. "Get the _____?"
7. A trying experience

ANSWER

TIPECO
SLIUO
FITRD
DALERO

DOWN

CLUE

1. Where royalty might live
2. Found in S. America
3. Influence, arouse
4. To do with the mind

ANSWER

CLEPAA
RODEAUC
SPINRIE
LAMTEN

CLUE: If you don't *take* this, you might *lose* it

BONUS

How to play Complete the crossword puzzle by looking at the clues and unscrambling the answers. When the puzzle is complete, unscramble the circled letters to solve the BONUS.

JUMBLE CROSSWORDS™

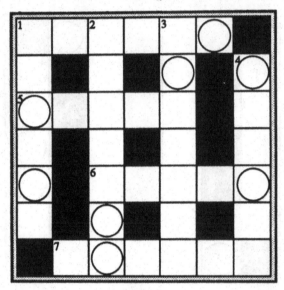

ACROSS

CLUE	ANSWER
1. Emotional condition	LAMERO
5. Having strong flavor	YAGNT
6. A fragrant flower	CLLAI
7. Hung around	STEDAY

DOWN

CLUE	ANSWER
1. Developed	EMTARU
2. A curled lock of hair	GINRTLE
3. Faithfully	YYLLAOL
4. Expressed	CIVOED

CLUE: This debuted in January of 1953

BONUS

How to play Complete the crossword puzzle by looking at the clues and unscrambling the answers. When the puzzle is complete, unscramble the circled letters to solve the BONUS.

JUMBLE CROSSWORDS™

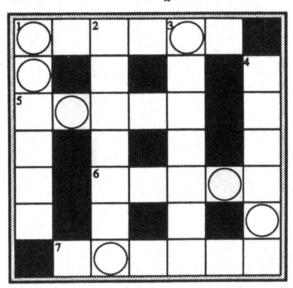

ACROSS

CLUE	ANSWER
1. Movie theater	MANICE
5. _____ away	DOTWE
6. Found in Nebraska	HAAMO
7. An uninterrupted series	KAESTR

DOWN

CLUE	ANSWER
1. Cows, steers	TELTAC
2. Scenic Rhode Island seaport	TRENPOW
3. Bring about an ageement	MITAEDE
4. Discover, reveal	USKMAN

CLUE: Handle

BONUS

How to play

Complete the crossword puzzle by looking at the clues and unscrambling the answers. When the puzzle is complete, unscramble the circled letters to solve the BONUS.

PUZZLE

#81

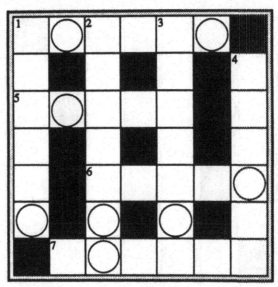

JUMBLE CROSSWORDS™

ACROSS

CLUE		ANSWER
1.	Not on the regular course	TANRER
5.	Helped	DDEIA
6.	Follow	DABIE
7.	Set up, planned	GADEST

DOWN

CLUE		ANSWER
1.	Pass by	PASEEL
2.	Bright with joy, happiness	TANDARI
3.	_____ off	DONGDIN
4.	Pal	FINRED

CLUE: Related to three *w*'s

BONUS

How to play — Complete the crossword puzzle by looking at the clues and unscrambling the answers. When the puzzle is complete, unscramble the circled letters to solve the BONUS.

JUMBLE CROSSWORDS™

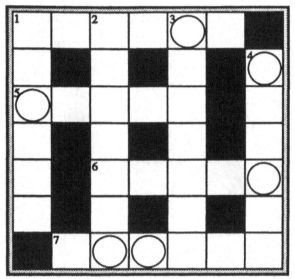

ACROSS

CLUE	ANSWER
1. Found in England	LODNNO
5. Used by an artist	SLEEA
6. Strict	GRIDI
7. Escaped	DUDEEL

DOWN

CLUE	ANSWER
1. Extra time or space	YAWELE
2. Found on the face	ONTSIRL
3. Done as a favor	GILDEOB
4. Insured	DONBED

CLUE: You can *see* in this manner

BONUS

How to play — Complete the crossword puzzle by looking at the clues and unscrambling the answers. When the puzzle is complete, unscramble the circled letters to solve the BONUS.

JUMBLE CROSSWORDS™

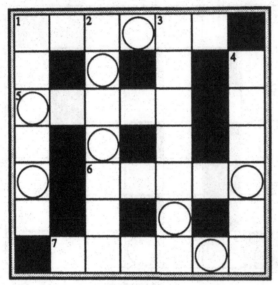

ACROSS

CLUE	ANSWER
1. Receive willingly	CACTEP
5. _____ area	ALRRU
6. You can open yours	TOMHU
7. Strange	WESCRY

DOWN

CLUE	ANSWER
1. Show up	VARRIE
2. Made from clay	CIMRAEC
3. Contaminate	ULETLOP
4. A number	HITGEY

CLUE: *Who cares?*

BONUS

How to play — Complete the crossword puzzle by looking at the clues and unscrambling the answers. When the puzzle is complete, unscramble the circled letters to solve the BONUS.

JUMBLE CROSSWORDS™

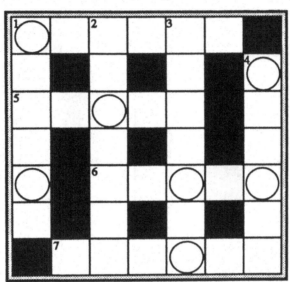

ACROSS

CLUE

1. Dangerous
5. Taunt
6. A temporary residence
7. Wet, marshy

ANSWER

SUNFAE
STEEA
GOLED
PAMWYS

DOWN

CLUE

1. A change for the better
2. _____ water
3. Political independence
4. A pastry factory

ANSWER

NUTRPU
LLSWOAH
ODEERMF
BYRKEA

CLUE: One corner of a *triangle*

BONUS

How to play — Complete the crossword puzzle by looking at the clues and unscrambling the answers. When the puzzle is complete, unscramble the circled letters to solve the BONUS.

JUMBLE CROSSWORDS™

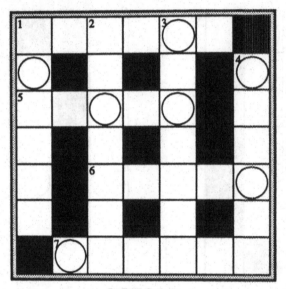

ACROSS

CLUE	ANSWER
1. Spoken rather than written	B L A R V E
5. An Arabian country	M E E Y N
6. Ranked	D A T E R
7. A type of *shower*	T E M E R O

DOWN

CLUE	ANSWER
1. Journey	G A V Y O E
2. Regret	E M E R S O R
3. A famous "Club" member	T A N E E N T
4. A large bird	C R O O N D

CLUE: This *chain* can be made of people

BONUS

How to play — Complete the crossword puzzle by looking at the clues and unscrambling the answers. When the puzzle is complete, unscramble the circled letters to solve the BONUS.

JUMBLE CROSSWORDS™

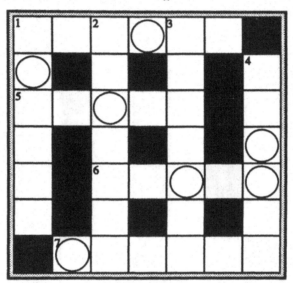

ACROSS

CLUE	ANSWER
1. It's alive, but has no organs	BAMEOA
5. Acknowledged	TENOD
6. _____ by _____	CIKRB
7. Eerie	PEYREC

DOWN

CLUE	ANSWER
1. An acting *Tom*	DONLAR
2. This is 31 days long	ROTBECO
3. Often earlier for children	TEEDBIM
4. In poor health	SYLKCI

CLUE: Players use bats when playing this

BONUS

How to play   Complete the crossword puzzle by looking at the clues and unscrambling the answers. When the puzzle is complete, unscramble the circled letters to solve the BONUS.

PUZZLE

#87

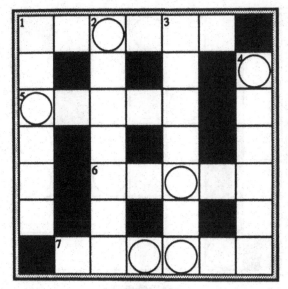

JUMBLE CROSSWORDS™

ACROSS

CLUE		ANSWER
1.	A European city	HURCIZ
5.	Stared	DAPEG
6.	The "Fighting _____"	SHRII
7.	Approach	DOTHEM

DOWN

CLUE		ANSWER
1.	A way to change direction	GAZZGI
2.	A classification of animals	PRETIEL
3.	A sea creature	SOCFDIH
4.	Verbally abused	BDAEHS

CLUE: An idea can be considered this

BONUS

How to play Complete the crossword puzzle by looking at the clues and unscrambling the answers. When the puzzle is complete, unscramble the circled letters to solve the BONUS.

88

JUMBLE CROSSWORDS™

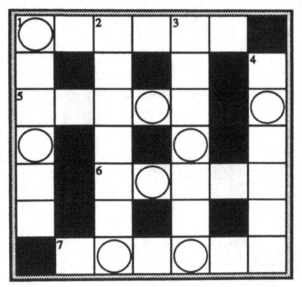

ACROSS

CLUE

1. Delivered
5. An illegal organization
6. A fabric
7. "Gary" is one in golf

ANSWER

DVERES
FIMAA
STNIA
YAPRLE

DOWN

CLUE

1. Try, test
2. Nonacceptance
3. "On the nose"
4. A black eye

ANSWER

PLAMSE
FERSLUA
YXETCLA
RINSEH

CLUE: An exam

BONUS

How to play — Complete the crossword puzzle by looking at the clues and unscrambling the answers. When the puzzle is complete, unscramble the circled letters to solve the BONUS.

JUMBLE CROSSWORDS™

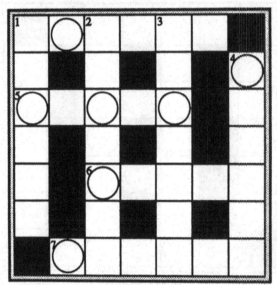

ACROSS

CLUE	ANSWER
1. Need to solve a problem	REEYDM
5. Blend	GEMRE
6. Not allowed in hockey	GINCI
7. A type of *hit*	LGENIS

DOWN

CLUE	ANSWER
1. Stay	MANERI
2. A drink	TIMRAIN
3. Counting your calories	GITNIDE
4. This can cause many deaths	PULGEA

CLUE: An assertion, basis for an argument

BONUS

How to play — Complete the crossword puzzle by looking at the clues and unscrambling the answers. When the puzzle is complete, unscramble the circled letters to solve the BONUS.

PUZZLE #90

JUMBLE CROSSWORDS™

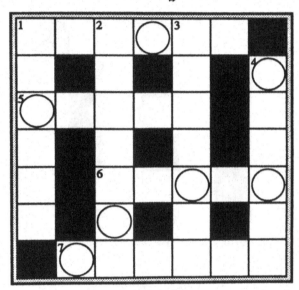

ACROSS

CLUE	ANSWER
1. "Wonder Years" star	AAEGVS
5. Level	YALRE
6. This relates to money	DERGE
7. Result of a large impact	TRACER

DOWN

CLUE	ANSWER
1. Worn as a result of injury	TIPSLN
2. A "Star Trek" series	GRAYOVE
3. A shirt is one	MRAGTEN
4. You can *cross* one	BREDRO

CLUE: An undesirable outcome

BONUS

How to play — Complete the crossword puzzle by looking at the clues and unscrambling the answers. When the puzzle is complete, unscramble the circled letters to solve the BONUS.

#91

JUMBLE CROSSWORDS™

ACROSS

CLUE	ANSWER
1. Sometimes played on grass	S T N N I E
5. A walkway	S L I A E
6. *Back* _____	S R D O A
7. This has no engine	R I G D E L

DOWN

CLUE	ANSWER
1. Warmed	W E T H A D
2. Part of a face	L I N R O T S
3. An island country	I L A D N E C
4. A quarterback is one	S P E S R A

CLUE: Last name of a famous actor, singer and driver

BONUS

How to play — Complete the crossword puzzle by looking at the clues and unscrambling the answers. When the puzzle is complete, unscramble the circled letters to solve the BONUS.

PUZZLE
#92

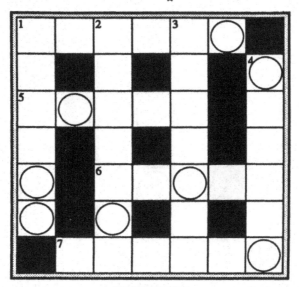

JUMBLE CROSSWORDS™

ACROSS

CLUE	ANSWER
1. An injury	NARPSI
5. Maintain, make like new	TIREF
6. Explode	PURTE
7. Clever, practical	SDWERH

DOWN

CLUE	ANSWER
1. Certainly	LERYUS
2. "_____ my memory"	HEERRSF
3. Enter when uninvited	TINDERU
4. Smashed in	TDDNEE

CLUE: Something might *appear* this way

BONUS

How to play: Complete the crossword puzzle by looking at the clues and unscrambling the answers. When the puzzle is complete, unscramble the circled letters to solve the BONUS.

JUMBLE® CROSSWORDS™

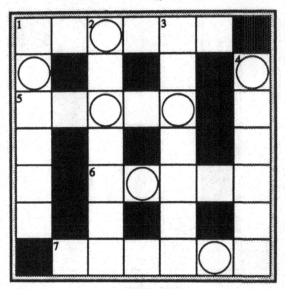

ACROSS

CLUE	ANSWER
1. A *situation* might be this	YIKCTS
5. Become smaller	PRATE
6. Often upstairs	CITAT
7. Pelted	NOTSDE

DOWN

CLUE	ANSWER
1. Sarcastic humor	RATSIE
2. Insert	TANMIPL
3. An insoluble protein	TAKRENI
4. Sticky, thick	SIVICD

CLUE: A word before *school, life* or *matter*

BONUS

How to play — Complete the crossword puzzle by looking at the clues and unscrambling the answers. When the puzzle is complete, unscramble the circled letters to solve the BONUS.

JUMBLE CROSSWORDS™

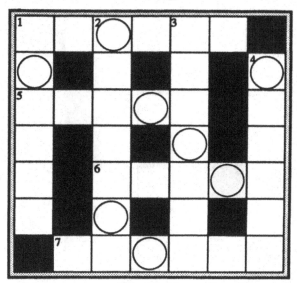

ACROSS

CLUE	ANSWER
1. A landlord's customer	TTNNAE
5. The thirteenth largest state	AIODH
6. Perry _____	SLILE
7. A state of inactivity	SSSAIT

DOWN

CLUE	ANSWER
1. A movement	WITHCT
2. Closest	STEERAN
3. These are often boiled	ONOLEDS
4. A type of survey	CSSUNE

CLUE: You might put one in a bag

BONUS

How to play Complete the crossword puzzle by looking at the clues and unscrambling the answers. When the puzzle is complete, unscramble the circled letters to solve the BONUS.

JUMBLE CROSSWORDS™

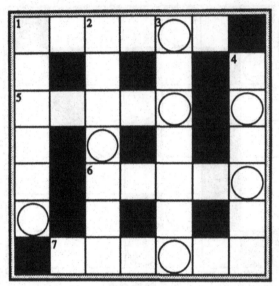

ACROSS

CLUE	ANSWER
1. Walk behind	WOLFLO
5. A dance	BAMRU
6. Usually green or black	VILOE
7. A puzzling person	EAMNGI

DOWN

CLUE	ANSWER
1. A *wheel* or a "Bueller"	REFSRI
2. "National _____"	PAMONOL
3. Speaking	GARONIT
4. A goddess	AANTEH

CLUE: A type of fee

BONUS

How to play Complete the crossword puzzle by looking at the clues and unscrambling the answers. When the puzzle is complete, unscramble the circled letters to solve the BONUS.

JUMBLE CROSSWORDS™

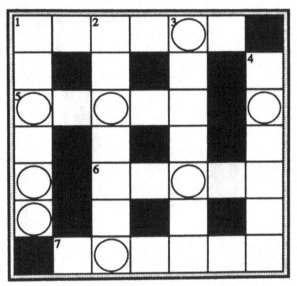

ACROSS

CLUE

1. Actor's instructions
5. _____ and operated
6. Incorrect
7. Chipped, shredded

ANSWER

TIPRCS
DOWNE
GORNW
KFALDE

DOWN

CLUE

1. Rocky
2. Sometimes a *notice*
3. It might come with a key
4. _____ the ball

ANSWER

MYTROS
NEERLAW
DKOCLAP
GHDEGO

CLUE: You might *go to jail* if you play this

BONUS

How to play

Complete the crossword puzzle by looking at the clues and unscrambling the answers. When the puzzle is complete, unscramble the circled letters to solve the BONUS.

#97

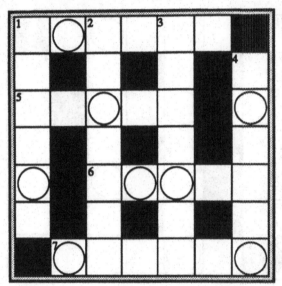

JUMBLE CROSSWORDS™

ACROSS

CLUE	**ANSWER**
1. Perfomed by sight alone	SLAVUI
5. *Earth's sister*	SNUEV
6. Edit	EDNME
7. A type of hot spring	SEGRYE

DOWN

CLUE	**ANSWER**
1. Actress *Vance*	NVAVII
2. Honest	CREENIS
3. A sore	SCABSSE
4. Nicer	RIKEDN

CLUE: This can cause severe pain

BONUS

How to play Complete the crossword puzzle by looking at the clues and unscrambling the answers. When the puzzle is complete, unscramble the circled letters to solve the BONUS.

JUMBLE CROSSWORDS™

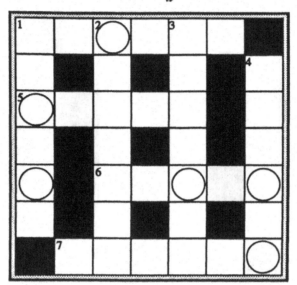

ACROSS

CLUE	ANSWER
1. Close	BYREAN
5. A singing "Brooks"	RATGH
6. Pointed	DIMEA
7. Layers	AATTRS

DOWN

CLUE	ANSWER
1. *Gold* _____	GUNTEG
2. Informed or side by side	STBRAAE
3. A former European kingdom	MBEOHAI
4. A treeless arctic plain	TRANDU

CLUE: A word before *control* or after *storm*

BONUS

How to play — Complete the crossword puzzle by looking at the clues and unscrambling the answers. When the puzzle is complete, unscramble the circled letters to solve the BONUS.

JUMBLE CROSSWORDS™

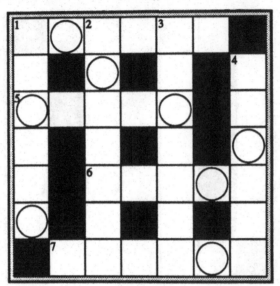

ACROSS

CLUE	ANSWER
1. 'Dennis' was one	MANEEC
5. A moon orbiting Saturn	TTNIA
6. This contains oxygen	ODXIE
7. Thin	NIKYNS

DOWN

CLUE	ANSWER
1. A rebellion	TUIMYN
2. A group, system	ROKTNWE
3. Deliver	SONGCIN
4. Well	YLECNI

CLUE: You may be prone to put this after *natural*

BONUS

How to play   Complete the crossword puzzle by looking at the clues and unscrambling the answers. When the puzzle is complete, unscramble the circled letters to solve the BONUS.

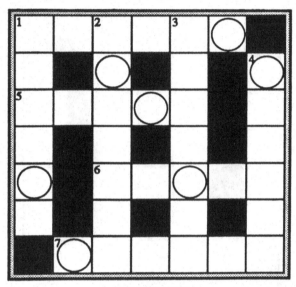

JUMBLE CROSSWORDS™

ACROSS

CLUE	ANSWER
1. The universe, everything	RANUTE
5. A type of meat	PIRTE
6. Live	SITEX
7. A mark of disgrace	GATMIS

DOWN

CLUE	ANSWER
1. A feeling	TONNOI
2. A three-pronged instrument	TIDRNET
3. You may "go" this if hit	GERLENI
4. A famous first lady	HATRAM

CLUE: A *broken* one may cause problems

BONUS

How to play Complete the crossword puzzle by looking at the clues and unscrambling the answers. When the puzzle is complete, unscramble the circled letters to solve the BONUS.

JUMBLE CROSSWORDS™

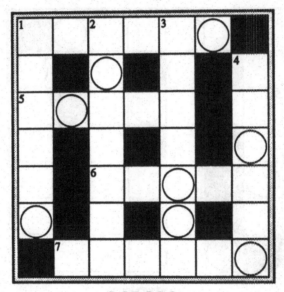

ACROSS

CLUE	ANSWER
1. Listed, scheduled	STALED
5. A dark time	GINTH
6. "Lee" or "Willis"	CURBE
7. To lean to one side	ECERAN

DOWN

CLUE	ANSWER
1. An ice cream dish	NEDUAS
2. A+B=C, etc.	AARLBGE
3. Excite	USHTEEN
4. Behind a ship	TASREN

CLUE: If a *number* is this, it will be harder to find

BONUS

How to play   Complete the crossword puzzle by looking at the clues and unscrambling the answers. When the puzzle is complete, unscramble the circled letters to solve the BONUS.

PUZZLE
#102

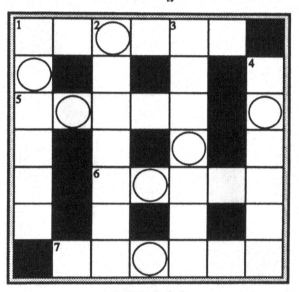

JUMBLE CROSSWORDS™

ACROSS

CLUE	ANSWER
1. A duty, charge	FATFIR
5. This person runs errands	REGFO
6. Associated with wealth	TEILE
7. A fictional bar	SHRECE

DOWN

CLUE	ANSWER
1. Pulled	GUTDEG
2. Revive	SHERREF
3. _____ soil	TREELIF
4. A high-ranking nun	BASESB

CLUE: It's hard to get *out* of this once you're *in* it

BONUS

How to play — Complete the crossword puzzle by looking at the clues and unscrambling the answers. When the puzzle is complete, unscramble the circled letters to solve the BONUS.

PUZZLE #103

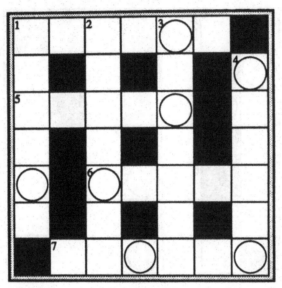

JUMBLE CROSSWORDS™

ACROSS

CLUE	ANSWER
1. A severe drop	GUPELN
5. A synthetic material	NNYOL
6. From Japan, India, etc.	AANIS
7. An indication of trouble	TTERHA

DOWN

CLUE	ANSWER
1. This has a sharp end	PLICNE
2. Let go, untie	SHUNALE
3. A reason to take cover	FINERUG
4. A poem	STNNOE

CLUE: *Low* ones may result in a cancellation

BONUS

How to play — Complete the crossword puzzle by looking at the clues and unscrambling the answers. When the puzzle is complete, unscramble the circled letters to solve the BONUS.

JUMBLE CROSSWORDS™

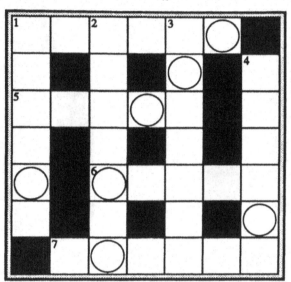

ACROSS

CLUE	ANSWER
1. A fictional "Bunker"	HARICE
5. A _____ day	AYRNI
6. Destroys	SKLIL
7. Battled with foils or sabers	CEEFDN

DOWN

CLUE	ANSWER
1. These have sharp ends	RARSWO
2. Similar to wrinkle	RICLEKN
3. Perfect	CLYLDII
4. Not open	SCLDEO

CLUE: A 7th and a 1st together equals one

BONUS

How to play — Complete the crossword puzzle by looking at the clues and unscrambling the answers. When the puzzle is complete, unscramble the circled letters to solve the BONUS.

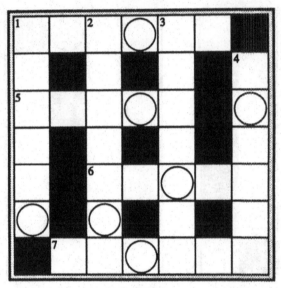

JUMBLE CROSSWORDS™

ACROSS

CLUE	ANSWER
1. Sneaky	FATRCY
5. A *late night* host	DDIVA
6. Actor *Henry*	VALIS
7. This bird likes fish	SYEORP

DOWN

CLUE	ANSWER
1. Begger	GADCRE
2. Recommends	SSEVDAI
3. A young child	TREDLDO
4. An *engine* or traffic circle	TRAOYR

CLUE: You may have to *keep* yours *low*

BONUS

How to play — Complete the crossword puzzle by looking at the clues and unscrambling the answers. When the puzzle is complete, unscramble the circled letters to solve the BONUS.

JUMBLE CROSSWORDS™

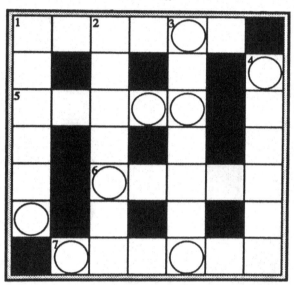

ACROSS

CLUE	ANSWER
1. An _____ joke	DNSEII
5. Actor *Raul's* last name	AJIUL
6. Ridges of coral, rocks, etc.	FERSE
7. Defeated	DETESB

DOWN

CLUE	ANSWER
1. A broken ankle is one	RUYNIJ
2. To go all out	SGRELUP
3. Most important	SETDRAE
4. Sheltered, protected	SHEDUO

CLUE: A reason to be *happy*

BONUS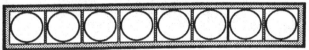

How to play   Complete the crossword puzzle by looking at the clues and unscrambling the answers. When the puzzle is complete, unscramble the circled letters to solve the BONUS.

#107

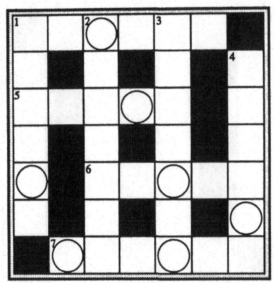

JUMBLE® CROSSWORDS™

ACROSS

CLUE	ANSWER
1. To speak softly, indistinctly	BEMLUM
5. Belonging to you	SYRUO
6. Contrary to the expected	RINOY
7. Bumper	DREENF

DOWN

CLUE	ANSWER
1. Needless violence	AEMMHY
2. A man's name	MACRIEU
3. Roped	SALOESD
4. Attorney	YRWLAE

CLUE: Independence

BONUS

How to play — Complete the crossword puzzle by looking at the clues and unscrambling the answers. When the puzzle is complete, unscramble the circled letters to solve the BONUS.

JUMBLE CROSSWORDS™

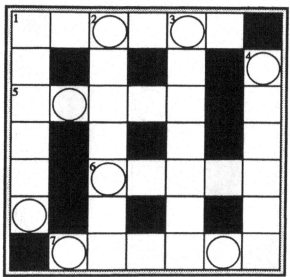

ACROSS

CLUE	ANSWER
1. Quick, without warning	TABPUR
5. The capital of Bulgaria	FOSAI
6. A Greek letter	PALAH
7. An unpleasant smell	HNESTC

DOWN

CLUE	ANSWER
1. Help	SSSTIA
2. Change direction	TRACFER
3. This is built for babies	LPPYANE
4. Unfasten	DTHCAE

CLUE: One side of this is often a picture

BONUS

How to play Complete the crossword puzzle by looking at the clues and unscrambling the answers. When the puzzle is complete, unscramble the circled letters to solve the BONUS.

#109

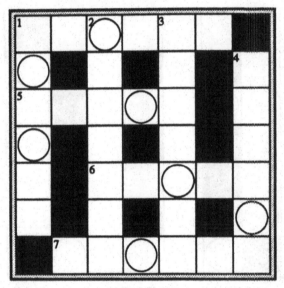

JUMBLE CROSSWORDS™

ACROSS

CLUE	ANSWER
1. Pick	COSHEO
5. You can *strike* one	THAMC
6. Similar to greased	LIDEO
7. Fragments	IESDRB

DOWN

CLUE	ANSWER
1. Widespread, general	MOCNOM
2. Result	METOOCU
3. A student	RASHCLO
4. A mass departure	DOXSUE

CLUE: This TV character was quite a character

BONUS

How to play — Complete the crossword puzzle by looking at the clues and unscrambling the answers. When the puzzle is complete, unscramble the circled letters to solve the BONUS.

PUZZLE

#110

JUMBLE CROSSWORDS™

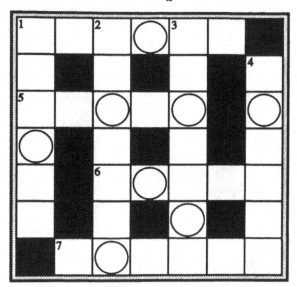

ACROSS

CLUE	ANSWER
1. Great	BREPUS
5. Egg-shaped	DOOIV
6. Manner	GUASE
7. This can be in *report* form	TTSSUA

DOWN

CLUE	ANSWER
1. In no hurry	WOLSYL
2. Multiplication's end result	TORDUPC
3. Bright with joy	DARNTIA
4. Used like *except*	SLENSU

CLUE: "Charlie's" last name

BONUS

How to play Complete the crossword puzzle by looking at the clues and unscrambling the answers. When the puzzle is complete, unscramble the circled letters to solve the BONUS.

 #111

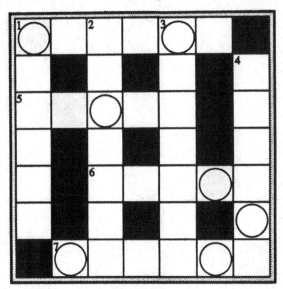

JUMBLE CROSSWORDS™

ACROSS

CLUE	ANSWER
1. Make	CATERE
5. Units of measurement	DARYS
6. A man's first name	SLIEL
7. A _____ apartment	ODUSTI

DOWN

CLUE	ANSWER
1. Weeping	CRINGY
2. Serious in intention	ASTERNE
3. Struggled	SESTULD
4. Complete failure	SCIFAO

CLUE: G.S. and R.E. to the movie business

BONUS

How to play — Complete the crossword puzzle by looking at the clues and unscrambling the answers. When the puzzle is complete, unscramble the circled letters to solve the BONUS.

JUMBLE CROSSWORDS™

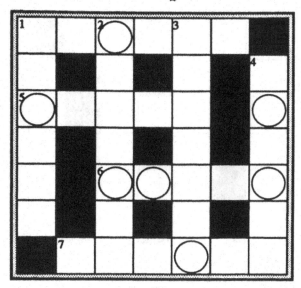

ACROSS

CLUE	ANSWER
1. A tool	CEWHNR
5. Rythmical stress	CUSTI
6. A TV waitress	CILAE
7. Cigar	GOTISE

DOWN

CLUE	ANSWER
1. Eight pounds, six ounces	THEWGI
2. Concentrate	TTXECAR
3. _____ call	CINTAGS
4. Hinder	PEEMDI

CLUE: Yours may vary

BONUS

How to play

Complete the crossword puzzle by looking at the clues and unscrambling the answers. When the puzzle is complete, unscramble the circled letters to solve the BONUS.

JUMBLE CROSSWORDS™

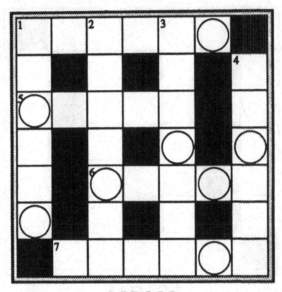

ACROSS

CLUE	ANSWER
1. To imitate	RYDAPO
5. Absolutely not	VENRE
6. A city	HAMOA
7. Comedian *Berle*	TIMNOL

DOWN

CLUE	ANSWER
1. Found in China	SAPADN
2. A food	VARLOII
3. Quiet	MADTONR
4. Territory	NAMDOI

CLUE: Similar looking but different, like *dash* and *dash*

BONUS

How to play — Complete the crossword puzzle by looking at the clues and unscrambling the answers. When the puzzle is complete, unscramble the circled letters to solve the BONUS.

JUMBLE CROSSWORDS™

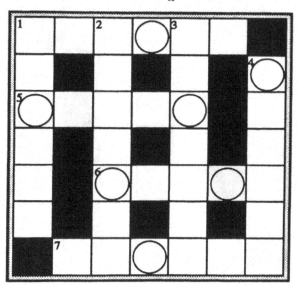

ACROSS

CLUE	ANSWER
1. Die	SPIRHE
5. Found in the sea	SMACL
6. A topic or a song	MEETH
7. Part of an atom	TORPNO

DOWN

CLUE	ANSWER
1. "Godfather" star	PINCAO
2. Nuclear _____	TRACROE
3. Surmise	STUPSCE
4. Window part	NECSER

CLUE: *"Cheers", "All in the Family", "Happy Days"*

BONUS

How to play   Complete the crossword puzzle by looking at the clues and
unscrambling the answers. When the puzzle is complete,
unscramble the circled letters to solve the BONUS.

 #115

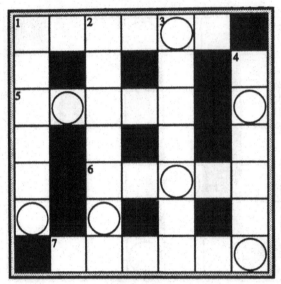

ACROSS

CLUE	ANSWER
1. A European capital	NIVEAN
5. Rabbit fur	PALNI
6. Frequently	NOTFE
7. Intensely	PYDELE

DOWN

CLUE	ANSWER
1. Important	ALVEDU
2. Examine *possibilities*	LEROPXE
3. Direct	NOONPTS
4. Crude housing	NTHYSA

CLUE: Found along the side of a road

BONUS

How to play — Complete the crossword puzzle by looking at the clues and unscrambling the answers. When the puzzle is complete, unscramble the circled letters to solve the BONUS.

JUMBLE® CROSSWORDS™

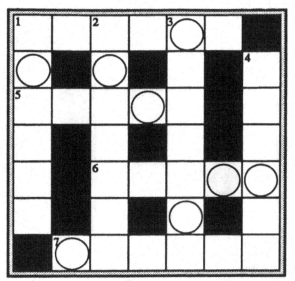

ACROSS

CLUE	ANSWER
1. Home to a famous harbor	O O N S T B
5. Separated	T A P R A
6. A mass of metal	T I N G O
7. The "Skipper's" boat	W I N N O M

DOWN

CLUE	ANSWER
1. Found in hair	S I B R D A
2. A Bantu language	H I I A W S L
3. This has many sides	T A G O O N C
4. Give	O W S T E B

CLUE: You are always waiting for this

BONUS

How to play   Complete the crossword puzzle by looking at the clues and unscrambling the answers. When the puzzle is complete, unscramble the circled letters to solve the BONUS.

 #117

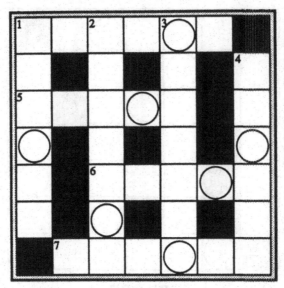

JUMBLE CROSSWORDS™

ACROSS

CLUE	ANSWER
1. "Monty _____"	NYPTHO
5. A saying	GAAED
6. A degree or stage	OTINP
7. Used in a laboratory	KEERBA

DOWN

CLUE	ANSWER
1. These are 'Great'	SNAPIL
2. Tread heavily	PARTLEM
3. Four-sided tapering shaft	OKSILEB
4. A trusted counselor	TREMON

CLUE: A fictional warrior race

BONUS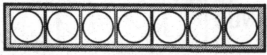

How to play — Complete the crossword puzzle by looking at the clues and unscrambling the answers. When the puzzle is complete, unscramble the circled letters to solve the BONUS.

PUZZLE

#118

JUMBLE CROSSWORDS™

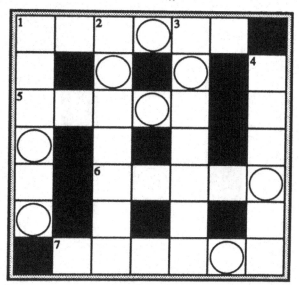

ACROSS

CLUE	ANSWER
1. The "Grim _____"	PEARER
5. Building materials	SGOLE
6. Actress *Moorehead*	SNAGE
7. Move upward	DEANCS

DOWN

CLUE	ANSWER
1. A type of *pitcher*	FILERE
2. Blankets	AASNHGF
3. Basic nature	SSCEEEN
4. _____ *in or out*	HASPED

CLUE: *"Maude"* and *"Laverne and Shirley"*

BONUS

How to play — Complete the crossword puzzle by looking at the clues and unscrambling the answers. When the puzzle is complete, unscramble the circled letters to solve the BONUS.

119

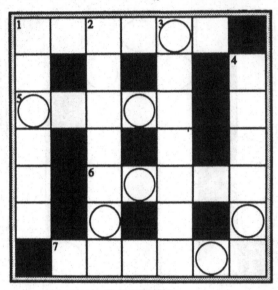

JUMBLE CROSSWORDS™

ACROSS

CLUE	ANSWER
1. Outdated, old-fashioned	SLIFSO
5. Taunt	STEEA
6. Means of access or *Bill*	STAGE
7. *Rich and _____*	MAEYRC

DOWN

CLUE	ANSWER
1. Coming hereafter	REFTUU
2. To astonish	GREATGS
3. A fixed condition	TINREAI
4. Stiff and brittle	SPYIRC

CLUE: A crossword puzzle is one

BONUS

How to play   Complete the crossword puzzle by looking at the clues and unscrambling the answers. When the puzzle is complete, unscramble the circled letters to solve the BONUS.

#120

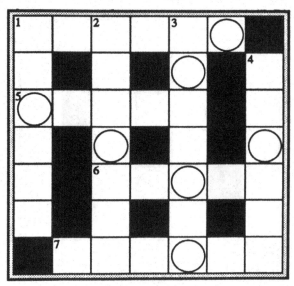

ACROSS

CLUE	ANSWER
1. Carve, model, weld	STCLUP
5. Bad	YSLUO
6. Counted people	SSREU
7. Dishes	TALPSE

DOWN

CLUE	ANSWER
1. Containing sodium chloride	STAEDL
2. Different	NUUUSLA
3. Make a _____	TANPYEM
4. Written in college	STSHIE

CLUE: Home to the brothers *Crane*

BONUS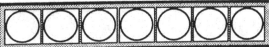

How to play — Complete the crossword puzzle by looking at the clues and unscrambling the answers. When the puzzle is complete, unscramble the circled letters to solve the BONUS.

 #121

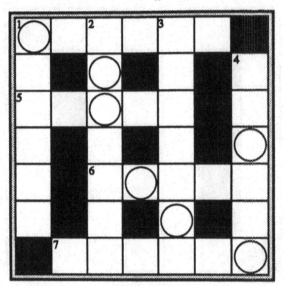

ACROSS

CLUE	ANSWER
1. Disappear	SVHNAI
5. Lacking in experience	NVAIE
6. Lift and throw with effort	AEEHV
7. Puts down on paper	STIREW

DOWN

CLUE	ANSWER
1. An Italian seaport	CINEVE
2. Not either	THERNIE
3. *Rod* _____	WESTTAR
4. A break	SCEERS

CLUE: A tennis *first* or *second*

BONUS

How to play   Complete the crossword puzzle by looking at the clues and unscrambling the answers. When the puzzle is complete, unscramble the circled letters to solve the BONUS.

JUMBLE CROSSWORDS™

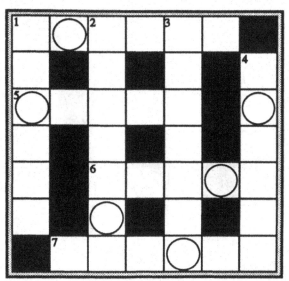

ACROSS

CLUE	ANSWER
1. A type of grasshopper	S T U O L C
5. A singing *Chapman*	C Y T A R
6. *Kent's* first name	R A L C K
7. Promise	G E P D E L

DOWN

CLUE	ANSWER
1. *Chicken* _____	L E T I T L
2. The space around an altar	L E C N H C A
3. Up	D A Y W R K S
4. A predicament	P E L K C I

CLUE: This person played this puzzle before you did

BONUS

How to play — Complete the crossword puzzle by looking at the clues and unscrambling the answers. When the puzzle is complete, unscramble the circled letters to solve the BONUS.

JUMBLE CROSSWORDS™

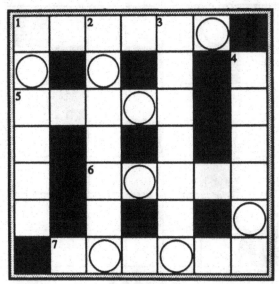

ACROSS

CLUE	ANSWER
1. A division of GM	N S T U A R
5. A famous poem	D I I A L
6. Pleasures	K S K I C
7. Taken	N E T S L O

DOWN

CLUE	ANSWER
1. Grinned	S L D I M E
2. A dense growth of shrubs	T T C H K E I
3. Extreme	C L A D I R A
4. Think	S N A R E O

CLUE: After *George* or *Linda*, or before *Bermuda*

BONUS

How to play — Complete the crossword puzzle by looking at the clues and unscrambling the answers. When the puzzle is complete, unscramble the circled letters to solve the BONUS.

JUMBLE CROSSWORDS™

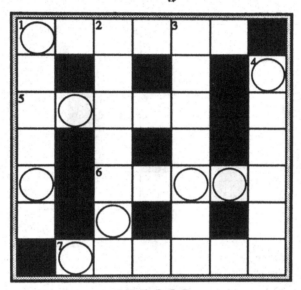

ACROSS

CLUE	ANSWER
1. The whole world	BLOGLA
5. Performer	OTRAC
6. Irritated	TYCHI
7. Used to boil water	TEKLET

DOWN

CLUE	ANSWER
1. A defensive *position*	LAIGOE
2. Indicate main features	NITLOEU
3. This grows on a tree	TRIPACO
4. A protein from living cells	MEEZNY

CLUE: A bank service that is sometimes *free*

BONUS

How to play — Complete the crossword puzzle by looking at the clues and unscrambling the answers. When the puzzle is complete, unscramble the circled letters to solve the BONUS.

PUZZLE

#125

JUMBLE CROSSWORDS™

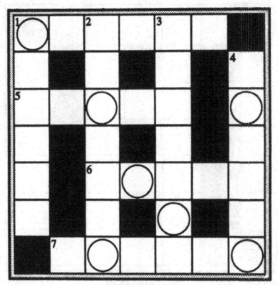

ACROSS

CLUE	ANSWER
1. Flaw	FEEDTC
5. _____ positive	PORFO
6. A Celtic language	SHIIR
7. He died in 44 B.C.	AAESRC

DOWN

CLUE	ANSWER
1. Neat, trim, smart	PADEPR
2. A character from "Maude"	DARLIOF
3. These get buried	SNCFFIO
4. Collect	GREHTA

CLUE: A very small country

BONUS

How to play — Complete the crossword puzzle by looking at the clues and unscrambling the answers. When the puzzle is complete, unscramble the circled letters to solve the BONUS.

126

#126

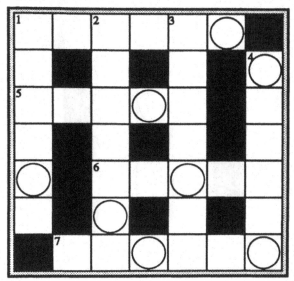

JUMBLE CROSSWORDS™

ACROSS

CLUE	ANSWER
1. Reason to get the vacuum	BRUMSC
5. If it's "red," it's serious	TRALE
6. Increase in amount	SARIE
7. 'The _____ Dog'	HGYSAG

DOWN

CLUE	ANSWER
1. Returned money	GANHEC
2. Dig up	TRANEUH
3. _____ suit	GITHNAB
4. That is to say; specifically	MANLEY

CLUE: A sea creature or a car

BONUS

How to play Complete the crossword puzzle by looking at the clues and unscrambling the answers. When the puzzle is complete, unscramble the circled letters to solve the BONUS.

JUMBLE CROSSWORDS™

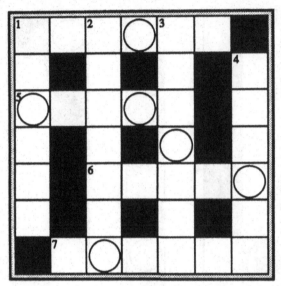

ACROSS

CLUE		ANSWER
1.	A type of bottle	FAREAC
5.	You can *make* these	SWEAV
6.	*St.* _____	SIOLU
7.	Find, uncover	TEEDTC

DOWN

CLUE		ANSWER
1.	A style of *hat*	BOCYOW
2.	Rotate	VVERLOE
3.	A narrow groove	SUSREFI
4.	A place to hang a coat	STOELC

CLUE: This works like a scale

BONUS

How to play   Complete the crossword puzzle by looking at the clues and unscrambling the answers. When the puzzle is complete, unscramble the circled letters to solve the BONUS.

JUMBLE®
CROSSWORDS

MASTER PUZZLES

PUZZLE #128

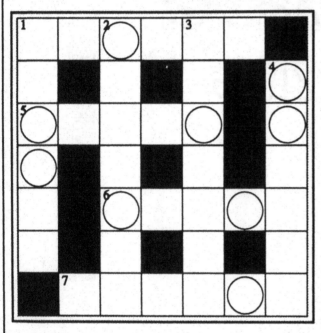

ACROSS

CLUE	ANSWER
1. A reappearance	CEENRO
5. Revolutions	STRUN
6. *Red* _____	TRALE
7. Cornered	AELDNG

DOWN

CLUE	ANSWER
1. One or the other	HEETIR
2. Positive	TRCNIAE
3. A city in Kansas	LSLSERU
4. Secured, based	TDEORO

How to play

Complete the crossword puzzle by looking at the clues and unscrambling the answers. When the puzzle is complete, unscramble the circled letters to solve the BONUS.

CLUE: This group is sometimes famous for its leader

BONUS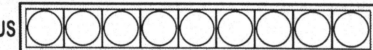

130

JUMBLE CROSSWORDS™

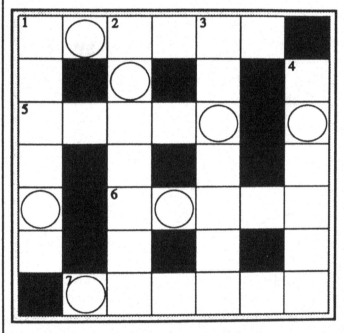

ACROSS

CLUE	ANSWER
1. A De Niro film	OAINCS
5. Thrown	GUNLS
6. Event area	AANER
7. Improve	TRBTEE

DOWN

CLUE	ANSWER
1. Fortified residence	CETLAS
2. Seasoned meat	GSSAAEU
3. Disregard	CTENGEL
4. Make up for, remedy	RRIEAP

How to play

Complete the crossword puzzle by looking at the clues and unscrambling the answers. When the puzzle is complete, unscramble the circled letters to solve the BONUS.

CLUE: "If x = 5 and y = 2, then x - y = 3" for example

BONUS

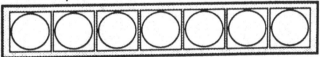

JUMBLE CROSSWORDS™

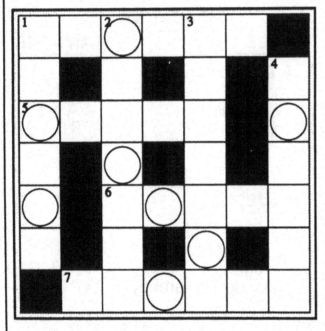

ACROSS

CLUE	ANSWER
1. An *"attractive"* person	T A G E N M
5. Fight	P A C R S
6. _____ surface	L A N R U
7. Students	S T A C E D

DOWN

CLUE	ANSWER
1. *"You _____ out"*	S M D I E S
2. Anthropoid ape	L I G R O A L
3. Great extent	S A P X E E N
4. _____ *fruit*	T S C I U R

How to play

Complete the crossword puzzle by looking at the clues and unscrambling the answers. When the puzzle is complete, unscramble the circled letters to solve the BONUS.

CLUE: One reason to wear a hat and glasses

BONUS

JUMBLE CROSSWORDS™

ACROSS

CLUE		ANSWER
1.	Pleasing	HYTCCA
5.	Long tailed bird	AAWCM
6.	Resemble	RAOVF
7.	Religious figure	CCILRE

DOWN

CLUE		ANSWER
1.	Active fighting	TOMBCA
2.	Diplomatic	CFUTLAT
3.	Nevertheless	VEOEHRW
4.	_____ acid	RNCIIT

How to play

Complete the crossword puzzle by looking at the clues and unscrambling the answers. When the puzzle is complete, unscramble the circled letters to solve the BONUS.

CLUE: "(3 + 8 - 1 + 2) × 2 + 1 = 36" for example

BONUS

PUZZLE #132

JUMBLE CROSSWORDS™

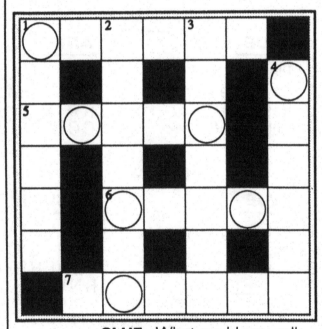

ACROSS

CLUE	ANSWER
1. *Zevon's* first name	REWANR
5. _____ *shark*	GRITE
6. An *eye* for example	ONARG
7. An arachnid	EPIRDS

DOWN

CLUE	ANSWER
1. Lose vitality	TRHEWI
2. Reorganize	RPUEORG
3. Angry	ANGERDE
4. *Ted* or *Janine*	TREUNR

CLUE: What could you call
Elizabeth and *Victoria*, and *Edward* and *George?*

BONUS
2 WORDS

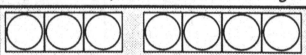

How to play

Complete the crossword puzzle by looking at the clues and unscrambling the answers. When the puzzle is complete, unscramble the circled letters to solve the BONUS.

134

JUMBLE CROSSWORDS™

ACROSS

CLUE	ANSWER
1. Small hole	TEEELY
5. This "was enough" in '77	HITGE
6. Dazzling effect	TACLE
7. *Island* "Prince"	WDDREA

DOWN

CLUE	ANSWER
1. Come into being	EGRMEE
2. Intellectual	GEDGAEH
3. Woman's name	ETLALSE
4. Happy	TEALED

How to play

Complete the crossword puzzle by looking at the clues and unscrambling the answers. When the puzzle is complete, unscramble the circled letters to solve the BONUS.

CLUE: *"You don't know how hard it was to make all the answers _____ _____ _*

BONUS
3 WORDS

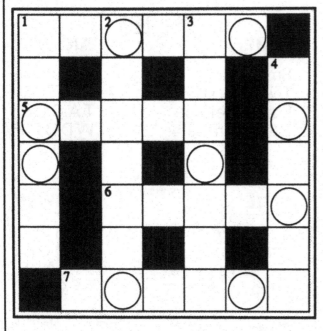

ACROSS

CLUE		ANSWER
1.	More than adequate	TYNLEP
5.	*Cara's* first name	EEINR
6.	"_____ Fudd"	REMEL
7.	Slowing or stoppage	SSSIAT

DOWN

CLUE		ANSWER
1.	_____ *Edward Island*	CIPENR
2.	Famous mountain	VEEETSR
3.	Type of container	ORTMHSE
4.	A "Ford"	STARUU

CLUE: Plans

BONUS

How to play

Complete the crossword puzzle by looking at the clues and unscrambling the answers. When the puzzle is complete, unscramble the circled letters to solve the BONUS.

JUMBLE CROSSWORDS™

ACROSS

CLUE		ANSWER
1.	Equal to six feet	MTOFAH
5.	*Robert _____ Stevenson*	USILO
6.	_____ *card*	PURTM
7.	Satisfactory	DETNEC

DOWN

CLUE		ANSWER
1.	Screen	LIFRET
2.	Appointed administrator	STRETUE
3.	Not clearly seen	OSEUCRB
4.	Elevated platform	PPTLIU

How to play

Complete the crossword puzzle by looking at the clues and unscrambling the answers. When the puzzle is complete, unscramble the circled letters to solve the BONUS.

CLUE: Exact

BONUS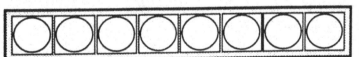

137

JUMBLE CROSSWORDS™

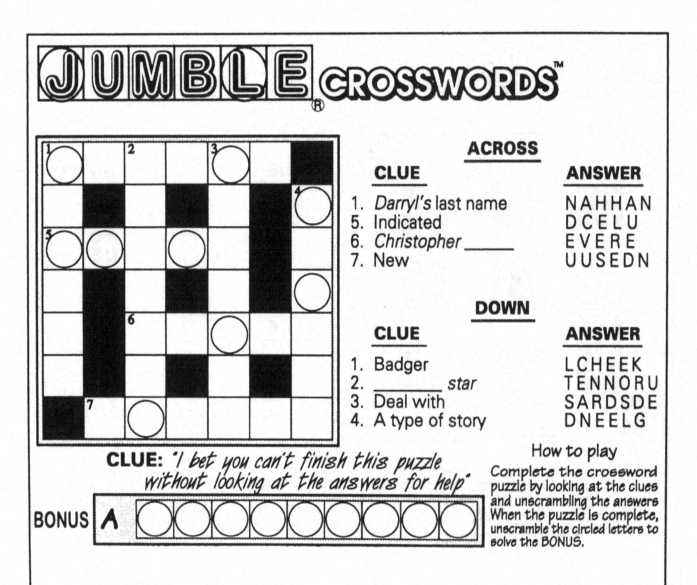

ACROSS

CLUE	ANSWER
1. *Darryl's* last name	NAHHAN
5. Indicated	DCELU
6. *Christopher* _____	EVERE
7. New	UUSEDN

DOWN

CLUE	ANSWER
1. Badger	LCHEEK
2. _____ star	TENNORU
3. Deal with	SARDSDE
4. A type of story	DNEELG

CLUE: *"I bet you can't finish this puzzle without looking at the answers for help"*

BONUS A ◯◯◯◯◯◯◯◯◯

How to play

Complete the crossword puzzle by looking at the clues and unscrambling the answers When the puzzle is complete, unscramble the circled letters to solve the BONUS.

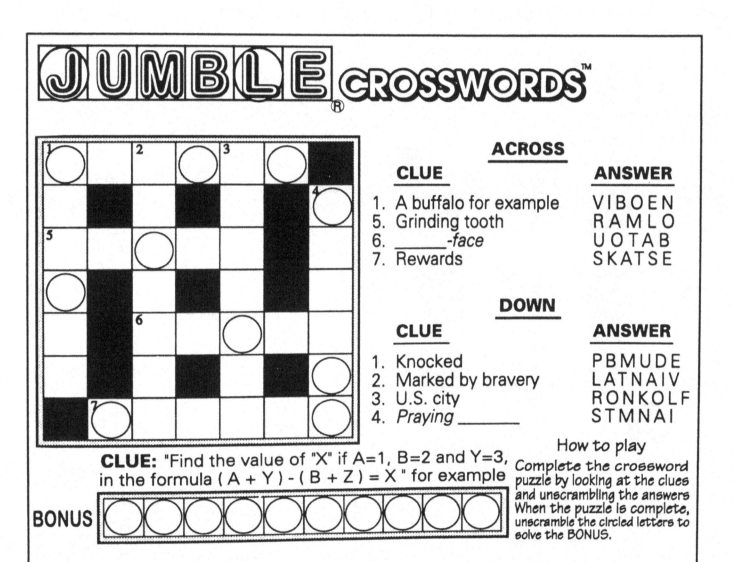

JUMBLE CROSSWORDS™

ACROSS

CLUE	ANSWER
1. A buffalo for example	V I B O E N
5. Grinding tooth	R A M L O
6. _____-face	U O T A B
7. Rewards	S K A T S E

DOWN

CLUE	ANSWER
1. Knocked	P B M U D E
2. Marked by bravery	L A T N A I V
3. U.S. city	R O N K O L F
4. *Praying* _____	S T M N A I

How to play

Complete the crossword puzzle by looking at the clues and unscrambling the answers When the puzzle is complete, unscramble the circled letters to solve the BONUS.

CLUE: "Find the value of "X" if A=1, B=2 and Y=3, in the formula (A + Y) - (B + Z) = X " for example

BONUS

JUMBLE CROSSWORDS™

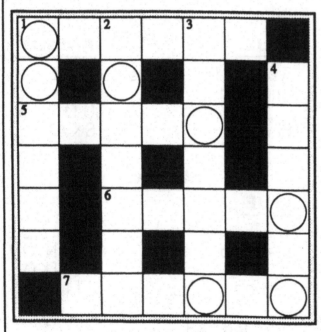

ACROSS

CLUE	ANSWER
1. *1, 5, 6 or 7* _____	SARSOC
5. Pester, annoy	TSEEA
6. Fatigued	RDTIE
7. Switched	DDTEAR

DOWN

CLUE	ANSWER
1. Song	MATENH
2. *Nuclear* _____	RROTAEC
3. Cut, cropped	DSEHRAE
4. Touched down	NALDDE

CLUE: A reason to turn around

BONUS
2 WORDS

How to play

Complete the crossword puzzle by looking at the clues and unscrambling the answers. When the puzzle is complete, unscramble the circled letters to solve the BONUS.

JUMBLE CROSSWORDS™

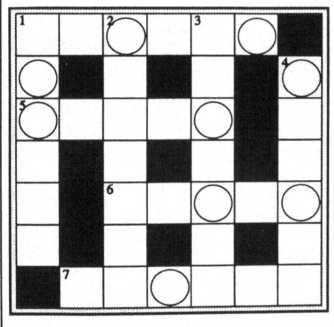

ACROSS

CLUE	ANSWER
1. Cupcake factory	R B E A K Y
5. *Flower* _____	L C H I D
6. Lawn	S G A R S
7. Incredible	A U E R L N

DOWN

CLUE	ANSWER
1. Quarrel	K I B C R E
2. "Worf" for example	G K I L O N N
3. To send out rays	D A R E T A I
4. Dangling ornament	S S A T L E

How to play

Complete the crossword puzzle by looking at the clues and unscrambling the answers. When the puzzle is complete, unscramble the circled letters to solve the BONUS.

CLUE: Its length is equivalent to 0.9144 of a meter

BONUS

#140

JUMBLE CROSSWORDS™

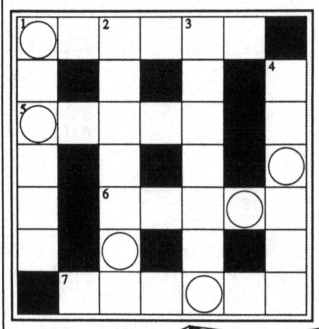

ACROSS

CLUE	ANSWER
1. More extensive	G R L A R E
5. Intense conflicts, events	M A D A R
6. *Mary _____ Moore*	L Y T R E
7. 6th of 7, or 5th of 5	D I R Y A F

DOWN

CLUE	ANSWER
1. Accounting book	E L G D R E
2. *Nuclear _____*	C A T E R R O
3. Empower	N A B D E E L
4. Turbulent	O T S M Y R

How to play

Complete the crossword puzzle by looking at the clues and unscrambling the answers. When the puzzle is complete, unscramble the circled letters to solve the BONUS.

CLUE:

BONUS

JUMBLE CROSSWORDS™

ACROSS

CLUE	ANSWER
1. *English* _____	NMIFUF
5. Heavy	TTUSO
6. Toughen	RENIU
7. Regret strongly	TAMNEL

DOWN

CLUE	ANSWER
1. Man	SIMRET
2. *Good Times* character	DORIALF
3. Cut in	ETINDUR
4. Choose	CEETLS

CLUE: *Jerry, Elaine,* and *George,* but not *Kramer,* on Seinfeld

BONUS
2 WORDS

How to play

Complete the crossword puzzle by looking at the clues and unscrambling the answers When the puzzle is complete, unscramble the circled letters to solve the BONUS.

PUZZLE #142

JUMBLE CROSSWORDS™

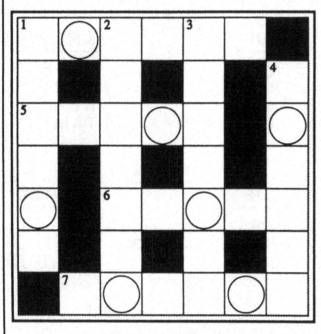

ACROSS

CLUE	ANSWER
1. A continent	RAACIF
5. Groundwork	SSIAB
6. Cast out	LIXEE
7. Position	CENATS

DOWN

CLUE	ANSWER
1. U.S. state capital	BAYNAL
2. Regard	TERCEPS
3. _____ Sea	ACPSINA
4. Stick	CEEHRO

How to play

Complete the crossword puzzle by looking at the clues and unscrambling the answers. When the puzzle is complete, unscramble the circled letters to solve the BONUS.

CLUE: Grisham's "The Client"

BONUS

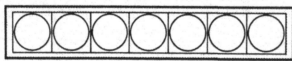

144

JUMBLE CROSSWORDS™

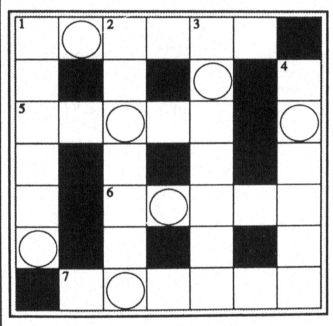

ACROSS

CLUE	ANSWER
1. Blueprint	M H E E C S
5. Fix	L E V S O
6. Closed in	T A G D E
7. Home to Luanda	N G O A A L

DOWN

CLUE	ANSWER
1. Method	T S S M E Y
2. Chlorine, for example	N L A H E G O
3. Musical title	R A M O S E T
4. *Bullock's* first name	N A S A R D

How to play

Complete the crossword puzzle by looking at the clues and unscrambling the answers. When the puzzle is complete, unscramble the circled letters to solve the BONUS.

CLUE: A source for data, information, facts, etc.

BONUS

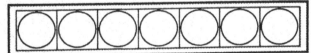

JUMBLE CROSSWORDS™

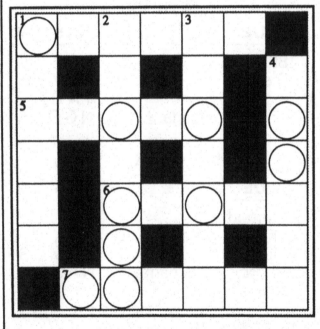

ACROSS

CLUE	ANSWER
1. Hereafter	FERUUT
5. *George's* last name	NEWTD
6. Central	RINEN
7. Orlando's location	DANLIN

DOWN

CLUE	ANSWER
1. Least	TEESWF
2. Stress	NEINOTS
3. Large round room	DUTNROA
4. Attained	OCSRED

CLUE: Literature classification

BONUS

How to play

Complete the crossword puzzle by looking at the clues and unscrambling the answers When the puzzle is complete, unscramble the circled letters to solve the BONUS.

JUMBLE CROSSWORDS™

ACROSS

CLUE		ANSWER
1.	Misfortune	SPHAIM
5.	Marked unevenness	PBMUS
6.	Greased	LODIE
7.	European city	NEEAGV

DOWN

CLUE		ANSWER
1.	U.S. city	LIBEOM
2.	Him or her	MOSNOEE
3.	Exculpate	SABEVOL
4.	Treeless plain	NUTRAD

How to play

Complete the crossword puzzle by looking at the clues and unscrambling the answers When the puzzle is complete, unscramble the circled letters to solve the BONUS.

CLUE: *Abbott* and *Costello*

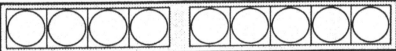

BONUS
2 WORDS

JUMBLE® CROSSWORDS™

ACROSS

CLUE	ANSWER
1. Series	GISTRN
5. In the course of	LOGNA
6. 13 - 19	SNETE
7. Depression	TACERR

DOWN

CLUE	ANSWER
1. Meager, scant	APSSER
2. Fowl variety	ORORETS
3. Disregard	NTCEELG
4. Computer pointer	URSCRO

How to play

Complete the crossword puzzle by looking at the clues and unscrambling the answers. When the puzzle is complete, unscramble the circled letters to solve the BONUS.

CLUE: Found in a Jumble puzzle

BONUS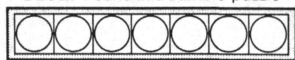

JUMBLE CROSSWORDS™

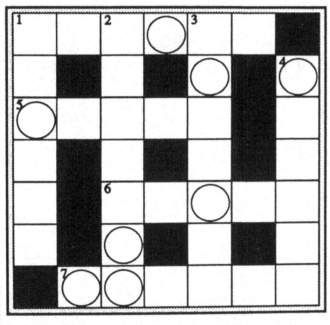

ACROSS

CLUE	ANSWER
1. Tell	LTETAT
5. Construction style	RODTU
6. Different	HOTRE
7. Planted	EDEDES

DOWN

CLUE	ANSWER
1. Names	STILET
2. Pond dweller	PTELAOD
3. Plunged, snapped	RULHECD
4. Scorch	RAESDE

How to play

Complete the crossword puzzle by looking at the clues and unscrambling the answers. When the puzzle is complete, unscramble the circled letters to solve the BONUS.

CLUE: *Columbia* and *Atlantis*

BONUS

 #148

JUMBLE® CROSSWORDS™

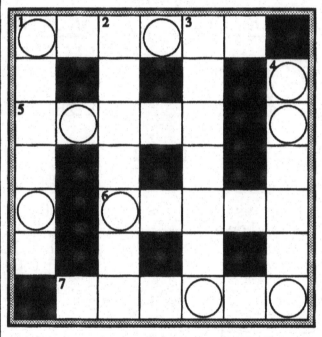

ACROSS

CLUE	ANSWER
1. Urge	TPPMOR
5. Temporary lodging	LOMET
6. Bar, billet, rod	GINTO
7. Williams' sport	TSNEIN

DOWN

CLUE	ANSWER
1. Wallop	UPMELM
2. Border	ONUELIT
3. Closed plane figure	PNOOGLY
4. Spiny plant	CTASCU

CLUE: Microsoft and IBM

BONUS

How to play

Complete the crossword puzzle by looking at the clues and unscrambling the answers. When the puzzle is complete, unscramble the circled letters to solve the BONUS.

JUMBLE CROSSWORDS™

ACROSS

CLUE	ANSWER
1. Part of the foot	STRAUS
5. Game name	MURYM
6. A crime	ANORS
7. *Third _____*	SPONRE

DOWN

CLUE	ANSWER
1. Small tower	RUTTER
2. Scour	REGAMUM
3. A president's first name	YLSUSES
4. Detective series	NNNOAC

How to play

Complete the crossword puzzle by looking at the clues and unscrambling the answers. When the puzzle is complete, unscramble the circled letters to solve the BONUS.

CLUE: "Unit"

BONUS ○○○○○○○○○

#150

JUMBLE CROSSWORDS™

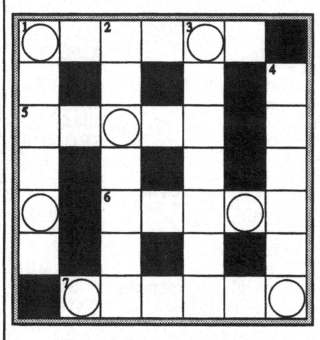

ACROSS

CLUE	ANSWER
1. Pummel, beat	PLAWOL
5. Storage area	ACTIT
6. Win over	RAMUN
7. Cleaned out	DDEEEW

DOWN

CLUE	ANSWER
1. Gun, knife	WNEPOA
2. Garden vegetable	TUTELEC
3. Tree farm	DROCHAR
4. Created, made	RFDEOM

How to play

Complete the crossword puzzle by looking at the clues and unscrambling the answers. When the puzzle is complete, unscramble the circled letters to solve the BONUS.

CLUE: This puzzle has all _____ _____ clues

BONUS 2 WORDS

JUMBLE CROSSWORDS™

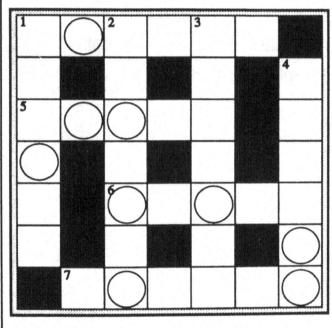

ACROSS

CLUE	ANSWER
1. N. American capital	WATAOT
5. Part of the U.A.E.	AIBUD
6. A slight error	SPALE
7. Connector	GRIDEB

DOWN

CLUE	ANSWER
1. Strange thing	TDODIY
2. Pipe shape	RBUTULA
3. Beaten	WPEIPDH
4. *Lorne's* last name	ENEGER

How to play

Complete the crossword puzzle by looking at the clues and unscrambling the answers. When the puzzle is complete, unscramble the circled letters to solve the BONUS.

CLUE: Plan

BONUS

JUMBLE CROSSWORDS™

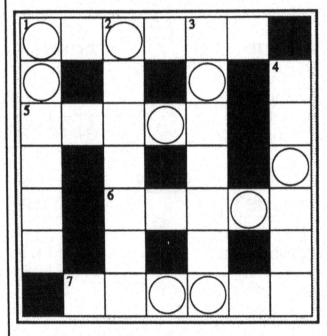

ACROSS

CLUE	ANSWER
1. *Bullock's* first name	N A S A R D
5. *Fine* _____	N I P T R
6. Despised	T H E A D
7. Scored	D D E R G A

DOWN

CLUE	ANSWER
1. Draw off, empty	H I S N O P
2. Also not	T E N R E I H
3. Turned around	O R E A T D T
4. Directed	U D I G D E

How to play

Complete the crossword puzzle by looking at the clues and unscrambling the answers. When the puzzle is complete, unscramble the circled letters to solve the BONUS.

CLUE: A country

BONUS

PUZZLE

#153

JUMBLE CROSSWORDS™

ACROSS

CLUE	ANSWER
1. *Madison* _____	C Y T O N U
5. Found in Florida	M M I I A
6. Coral island	L O T L A
7. *New* _____	C X I O E M

DOWN

CLUE	ANSWER
1. *Tailed* celestial bodies	S T O M C E
2. Ignorant	E U R N A W A
3. Found in Libya	T I L P O I R
4. Greek or Roman god	L A P O O L

How to play

Complete the crossword puzzle by looking at the clues and unscrambling the answers. When the puzzle is complete, unscramble the circled letters to solve the BONUS.

CLUE: Indonesia, Indiana and Baltimore

BONUS

155

JUMBLE® CROSSWORDS™

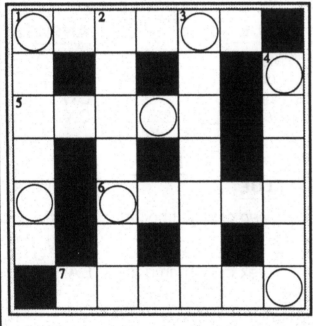

ACROSS

CLUE	ANSWER
1. Attract	PLEPAA
5. _____ inches or feet	BCCIU
6. A hockey no-no	GIINC
7. Sharp, wise	WRHSDE

DOWN

CLUE	ANSWER
1. Emphasis	TECACN
2. Issue	SHIBLUP
3. Attribute, assign	CABIRES
4. Pestered	GANDEG

How to play

Complete the crossword puzzle by looking at the clues and unscrambling the answers. When the puzzle is complete, unscramble the circled letters to solve the BONUS.

CLUE: A U.S. state

BONUS

#155

JUMBLE CROSSWORDS™

ACROSS

CLUE	ANSWER
1. To order back	M A D N E R
5. *The _____* (movie)	C R I L E
6. Proficient	T E A D P
7. A reason to hold hands	N A S E E C

DOWN

CLUE	ANSWER
1. Not commonly found	R R Y I A T
2. Usefulness	L I M E E G A
3. A very small particle	L U N C N O E
4. Found on a face	E G A T E O

CLUE: *This puzzle was much harder than yesterday's puzzle*

BONUS ○○○○○○○○○○

How to play

Complete the crossword puzzle by looking at the clues and unscrambling the answers When the puzzle is complete, unscramble the circled letters to solve the BONUS.

JUMBLE CROSSWORDS™

ACROSS

CLUE		ANSWER
1.	Subject	TMTARE
5.	An island	TEREC
6.	Dimension	REGAN
7.	Hurts	STAMRS

DOWN

CLUE		ANSWER
1.	A man's name	CIMEYK
2.	An accepted idea	HETROME
3.	*Rigby* or *Roosevelt*	AEELRON
4.	Muscles	SBPCIE

How to play

Complete the crossword puzzle by looking at the clues and unscrambling the answers. When the puzzle is complete, unscramble the circled letters to solve the BONUS.

CLUE: A city

BONUS

#157

JUMBLE CROSSWORDS™

ACROSS

CLUE	ANSWER
1. Dodged	D D K E C U
5. Confusion, problem	F U N A S
6. One that is gigantic	T T I N A
7. A card game	D R E B I G

DOWN

CLUE	ANSWER
1. Arid area	S E D R E T
2. Babble	A T H C R E T
3. Associated, likened	T U Q A E D E
4. Porous mass of fibers	O S P E N G

How to play

Complete the crossword puzzle by looking at the clues and unscrambling the answers When the puzzle is complete, unscramble the circled letters to solve the BONUS.

CLUE: Beginning

BONUS
2 WORDS

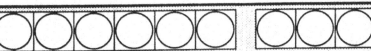

JUMBLE CROSSWORDS™

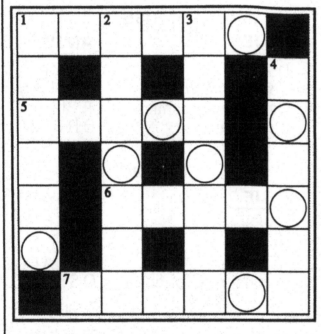

ACROSS

CLUE	ANSWER
1. Show off	NFULAT
5. An expression	MIIOD
6. Founded upon	SBEAD
7. Against	SERUVS

DOWN

CLUE	ANSWER
1. Stage _____	THRIGF
2. Agreeable	ABIMELA
3. Rival, opponent	MENIESS
4. A *suit*	DAPSSE

CLUE: Current

BONUS ◯◯ - ◯◯ - ◯◯◯◯

How to play

Complete the crossword puzzle by looking at the clues and unscrambling the answers. When the puzzle is complete, unscramble the circled letters to solve the BONUS.

#159

JUMBLE CROSSWORDS™

ACROSS

CLUE	ANSWER
1. A capital	WAATTO
5. Build, construct	SARIE
6. Pronounce, speak	TRUET
7. Safeguard	FEDNED

DOWN

CLUE	ANSWER
1. Stampede	RONSUH
2. Testimonial	BITEUTR
3. Grapple, scuffle	EWERLST
4. *William* or *Robert*	NODARC

CLUE: In need of money

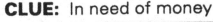

BONUS ◯◯◯◯ - ◯◯◯◯ - ◯◯◯

How to play

Complete the crossword puzzle by looking at the clues and unscrambling the answers When the puzzle is complete, unscramble the circled letters to solve the BONUS.

#160

JUMBLE CROSSWORDS™

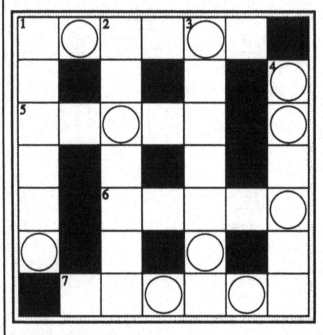

ACROSS

CLUE	ANSWER
1. Dangerous	FASENU
5. Produce, put on	GEAST
6. Summoned	DAPEG
7. A TV *Sherman*	PRETOT

DOWN

CLUE	ANSWER
1. Not spoken	AINDUS
2. A 1975 movie	OPASHMO
3. Goods, cargo	GRIFETH
4. Finance company	RLNEED

How to play

Complete the crossword puzzle by looking at the clues and unscrambling the answers When the puzzle is complete, unscramble the circled letters to solve the BONUS.

CLUE: Fewer than 50% of the population can make this claim

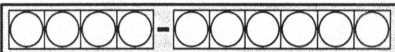

BONUS

JUMBLE CROSSWORDS™

ACROSS

CLUE	ANSWER
1. *Korman's* first name	EARVYH
5. Put back to zero	STERE
6. A hard quartz	NIFTL
7. Assert without proof	LGAELE

DOWN

CLUE	ANSWER
1. A social wasp	ORHENT
2. Relaxing	RLUEFTS
3. Become twisted	TENIWEN
4. Struggle	TABLTE

How to play

Complete the crossword puzzle by looking at the clues and unscrambling the answers When the puzzle is complete, unscramble the circled letters to solve the BONUS.

CLUE: Precedence

BONUS ○○○○○ - ○○ - ○○○

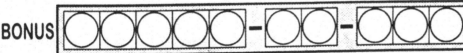

JUMBLE CROSSWORDS™

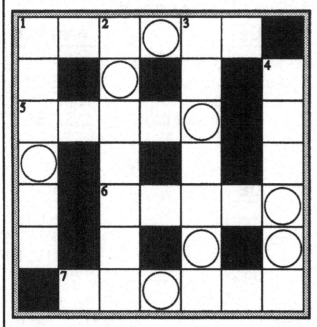

ACROSS

CLUE	ANSWER
1. Marked by furtiveness	AYNEKS
5. A Weaver movie	NILEA
6. Begins	SNOPE
7. Fashion	TEMDOH

DOWN

CLUE	ANSWER
1. Scorched	DRAEES
2. Occurrence	POEDSIE
3. A name	NHEETNK
4. Discontinued	SECDAE

How to play

Complete the crossword puzzle by looking at the clues and unscrambling the answers. When the puzzle is complete, unscramble the circled letters to solve the BONUS.

CLUE: Models

BONUS

JUMBLE CROSSWORDS™

ACROSS

CLUE	ANSWER
1. Undergo change	E E C O M B
5. Normal	S L U U A
6. To make smooth	N A P E L
7. Boring, dull	S Y G O T D

DOWN

CLUE	ANSWER
1. Batter, dent	R I B U E S
2. A round bread	M U R C T E P
3. A wild duck	L A M R A L D
4. Active	Y L I L E V

How to play

Complete the crossword puzzle by looking at the clues and unscrambling the answers. When the puzzle is complete, unscramble the circled letters to solve the BONUS.

CLUE: *"I love making these puzzles,"* for example

BONUS

JUMBLE CROSSWORDS™

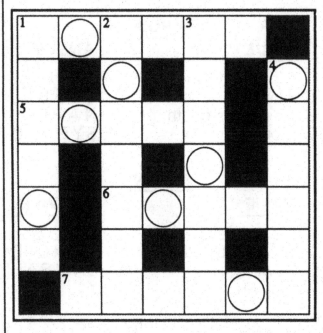

ACROSS

	CLUE	ANSWER
1.	A type of lizard	NAGUIA
5.	Small cabinet	THECS
6.	A type of competitor	RREAC
7.	Sunglasses	DASHSE

DOWN

	CLUE	ANSWER
1.	Stimulate	CETIIN
2.	Uncover	EUNHATR
3.	Observed	TONDEIC
4.	Brief advertisements	BSLBRU

How to play

Complete the crossword puzzle by looking at the clues and unscrambling the answers When the puzzle is complete, unscramble the circled letters to solve the BONUS.

CLUE: Certain

BONUS
3 WORDS

JUMBLE®
CROSSWORDS

DOUBLE BONUS
PUZZLES

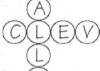

JUMBLE CROSSWORDS™

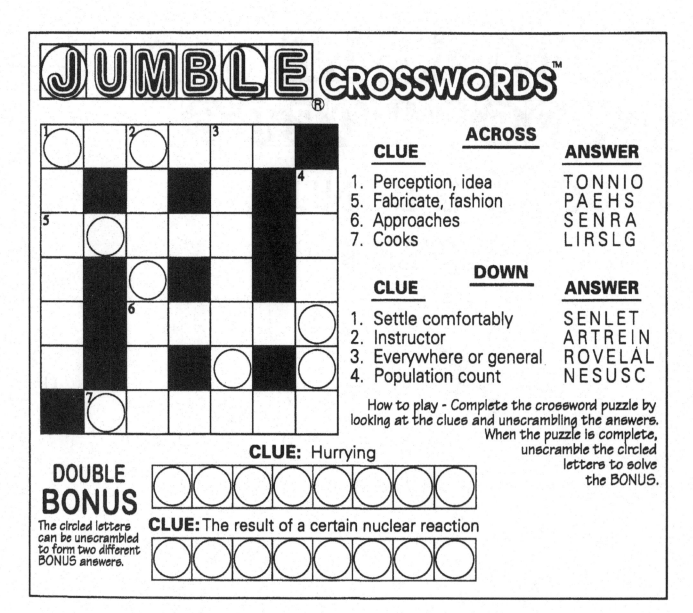

ACROSS

CLUE	ANSWER
1. Perception, idea	TONNIO
5. Fabricate, fashion	PAEHS
6. Approaches	SENRA
7. Cooks	LIRSLG

DOWN

CLUE	ANSWER
1. Settle comfortably	SENLET
2. Instructor	ARTREIN
3. Everywhere or general	ROVELAL
4. Population count	NESUSC

How to play - Complete the crossword puzzle by looking at the clues and unscrambling the answers. When the puzzle is complete, unscramble the circled letters to solve the BONUS.

CLUE: Hurrying

DOUBLE BONUS

The circled letters can be unscrambled to form two different BONUS answers.

CLUE: The result of a certain nuclear reaction

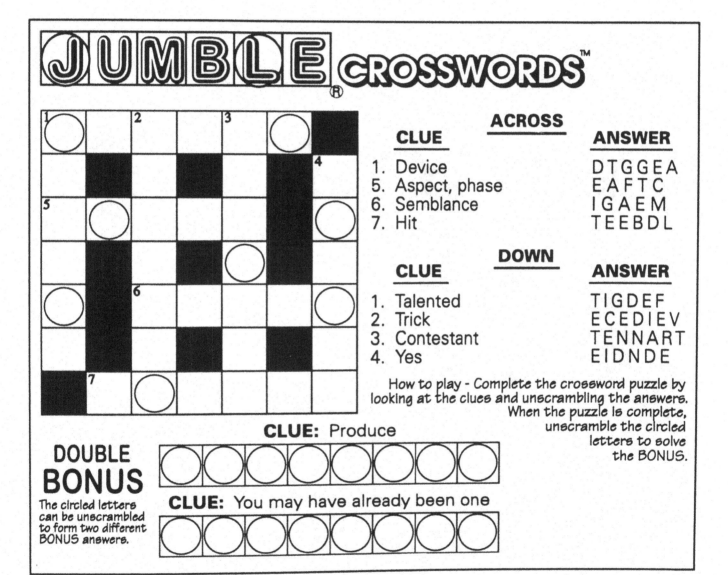

JUMBLE CROSSWORDS™

ACROSS

CLUE	ANSWER
1. Device	DTGGEA
5. Aspect, phase	EAFTC
6. Semblance	IGAEM
7. Hit	TEEBDL

DOWN

CLUE	ANSWER
1. Talented	TIGDEF
2. Trick	ECEDIEV
3. Contestant	TENNART
4. Yes	EIDNDE

How to play - Complete the crossword puzzle by looking at the clues and unscrambling the answers. When the puzzle is complete, unscramble the circled letters to solve the BONUS.

DOUBLE BONUS
The circled letters can be unscrambled to form two different BONUS answers.

CLUE: Produce

CLUE: You may have already been one

JUMBLE® CROSSWORDS™

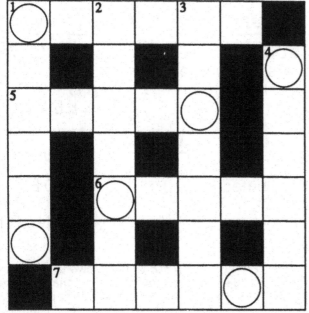

ACROSS

CLUE	ANSWER
1. *Weather* _____	P R E T O R
5. Himalayan mammal	N A P A D
6. A type of role	O A C E M
7. English physicist	O N N T E W

DOWN

CLUE	ANSWER
1. Pushes away	S L E R E P
2. Flamboyant style	C A N E P H A
3. Let back in	D M A E R I T
4. Tavern	N A S O L O

How to play - Complete the crossword puzzle by looking at the clues and unscrambling the answers. When the puzzle is complete, unscramble the circled letters to solve the BONUS.

DOUBLE BONUS

The circled letters can be unscrambled to form two different BONUS answers.

CLUE: 1, 5, 6 or 7 _____

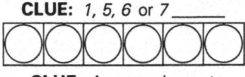

CLUE: An annual event

#168

JUMBLE CROSSWORDS™

ACROSS

CLUE	ANSWER
1. Plentiful	ALGREO
5. Close	HITTG
6. Carry along	GIBNR
7. Badger	CHEELK

DOWN

CLUE	ANSWER
1. Received	TOGNTE
2. Understandable	LLBIGEE
3. Consider again	ETRKHIN
4. Hang loosely	GEADNL

How to play - Complete the crossword puzzle by looking at the clues and unscrambling the answers. When the puzzle is complete, unscramble the circled letters to solve the BONUS.

DOUBLE BONUS
The circled letters can be unscrambled to form two different BONUS answers.

CLUE: Mystery person's status

CLUE: Understanding

171

JUMBLE® CROSSWORDS™

ACROSS

CLUE	ANSWER
1. Gregarious	C S L I A O
5. *Long Island* _____	N O D S U
6. Pace	P E T O M
7. A large city	Y Y E N D S

DOWN

CLUE	ANSWER
1. Sibling	T S S I R E
2. Bermuda, for example	C Y R O T U N
3. Found near the stomach	B M O E N D A
4. Bleak	L O G Y M O

How to play - Complete the crossword puzzle by looking at the clues and unscrambling the answers. When the puzzle is complete, unscramble the circled letters to solve the BONUS.

DOUBLE BONUS

The circled letters can be unscrambled to form two different BONUS answers.

CLUE: Inessential

CLUE: Reduced

#170

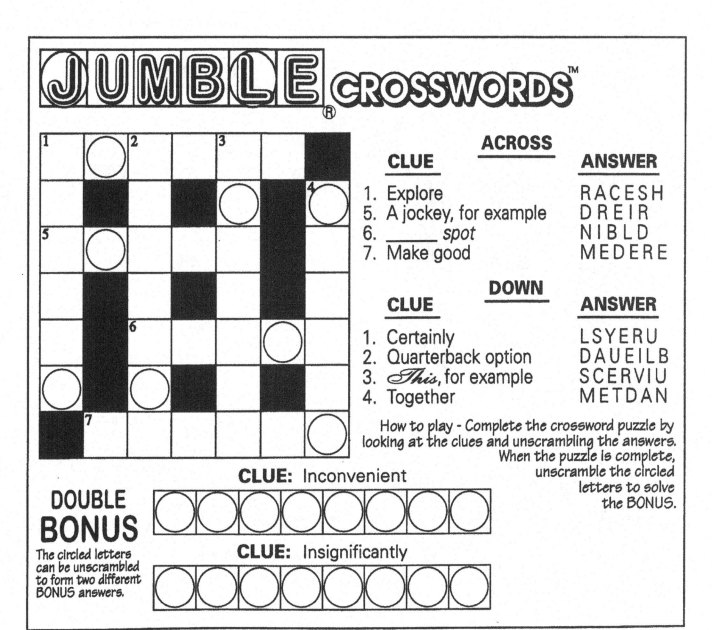

JUMBLE CROSSWORDS™

ACROSS

CLUE	ANSWER
1. Explore	RACESH
5. A jockey, for example	DREIR
6. _____ spot	NIBLD
7. Make good	MEDERE

DOWN

CLUE	ANSWER
1. Certainly	LSYERU
2. Quarterback option	DAUEILB
3. *This*, for example	SCERVIU
4. Together	METDAN

How to play - Complete the crossword puzzle by looking at the clues and unscrambling the answers. When the puzzle is complete, unscramble the circled letters to solve the BONUS.

DOUBLE BONUS

The circled letters can be unscrambled to form two different BONUS answers.

CLUE: Inconvenient

CLUE: Insignificantly

JUMBLE® CROSSWORDS™

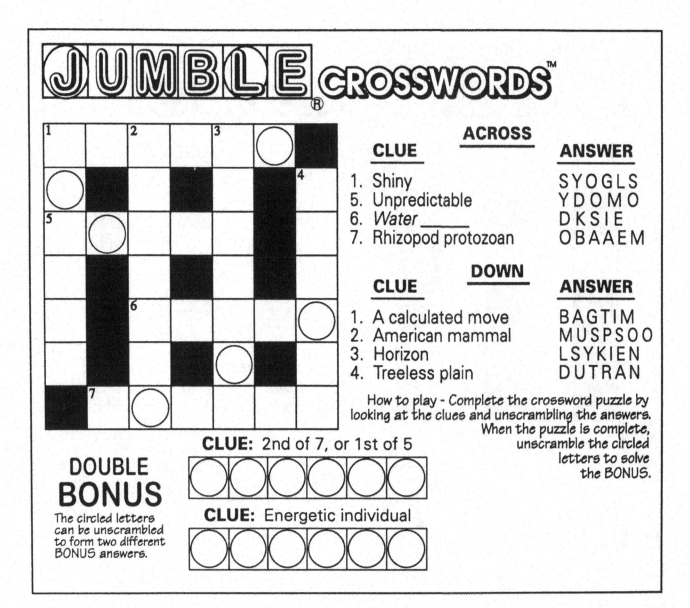

ACROSS

CLUE	ANSWER
1. Shiny	SYOGLS
5. Unpredictable	YDOMO
6. *Water* _____	DKSIE
7. Rhizopod protozoan	OBAAEM

DOWN

CLUE	ANSWER
1. A calculated move	BAGTIM
2. American mammal	MUSPSOO
3. Horizon	LSYKIEN
4. Treeless plain	DUTRAN

How to play - Complete the crossword puzzle by looking at the clues and unscrambling the answers. When the puzzle is complete, unscramble the circled letters to solve the BONUS.

DOUBLE BONUS

The circled letters can be unscrambled to form two different BONUS answers.

CLUE: 2nd of 7, or 1st of 5

◯ ◯ ◯ ◯ ◯ ◯

CLUE: Energetic individual

◯ ◯ ◯ ◯ ◯ ◯

#172

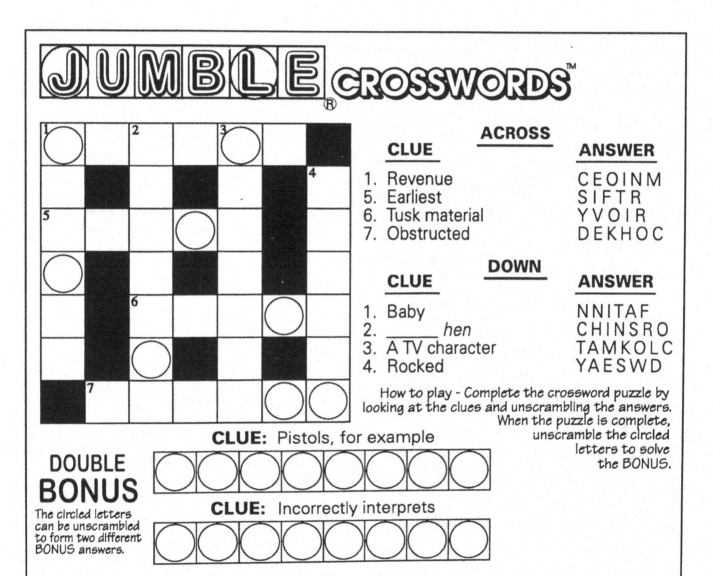

JUMBLE CROSSWORDS™

ACROSS

CLUE	ANSWER
1. Revenue	CEOINM
5. Earliest	SIFTR
6. Tusk material	YVOIR
7. Obstructed	DEKHOC

DOWN

CLUE	ANSWER
1. Baby	NNITAF
2. _____ hen	CHINSRO
3. A TV character	TAMKOLC
4. Rocked	YAESWD

How to play - Complete the crossword puzzle by looking at the clues and unscrambling the answers. When the puzzle is complete, unscramble the circled letters to solve the BONUS.

CLUE: Pistols, for example

DOUBLE BONUS

The circled letters can be unscrambled to form two different BONUS answers.

CLUE: Incorrectly interprets

#173

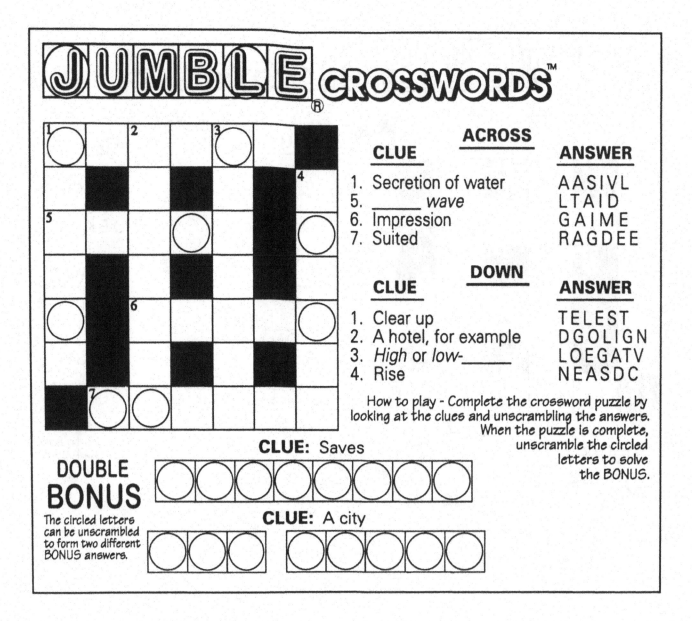

JUMBLE CROSSWORDS™

ACROSS

CLUE	ANSWER
1. Secretion of water	A A S I V L
5. _____ wave	L T A I D
6. Impression	G A I M E
7. Suited	R A G D E E

DOWN

CLUE	ANSWER
1. Clear up	T E L E S T
2. A hotel, for example	D G O L I G N
3. High or low-_____	L O E G A T V
4. Rise	N E A S D C

How to play - Complete the crossword puzzle by looking at the clues and unscrambling the answers. When the puzzle is complete, unscramble the circled letters to solve the BONUS.

CLUE: Saves

DOUBLE BONUS
The circled letters can be unscrambled to form two different BONUS answers.

CLUE: A city

JUMBLE CROSSWORDS™

ACROSS

CLUE	ANSWER
1. Slicer	R U T C E T
5. Avoid	G E D D O
6. Home to approx. 330,000	A A H O M
7. Car accessory	T H E E R A

DOWN

CLUE	ANSWER
1. Snuggle	L E D U C D
2. A type of amphibian	P A T D E L O
3. Stately	G E E N T L A
4. Matter	F F R I A A

How to play - Complete the crossword puzzle by looking at the clues and unscrambling the answers. When the puzzle is complete, unscramble the circled letters to solve the BONUS.

DOUBLE BONUS

The circled letters can be unscrambled to form two different BONUS answers.

CLUE: Your bank might be yours

CLUE: Stone, for example

177

#175

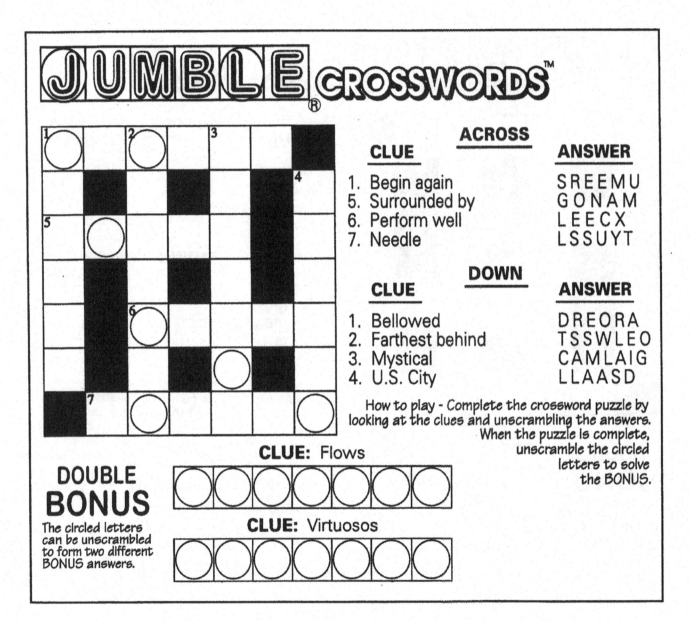

JUMBLE® CROSSWORDS™

ACROSS

CLUE	ANSWER
1. Begin again	SREEMU
5. Surrounded by	GONAM
6. Perform well	LEECX
7. Needle	LSSUYT

DOWN

CLUE	ANSWER
1. Bellowed	DREORA
2. Farthest behind	TSSWLEO
3. Mystical	CAMLAIG
4. U.S. City	LLAASD

How to play - Complete the crossword puzzle by looking at the clues and unscrambling the answers. When the puzzle is complete, unscramble the circled letters to solve the BONUS.

CLUE: Flows

DOUBLE BONUS

The circled letters can be unscrambled to form two different BONUS answers.

CLUE: Virtuosos

JUMBLE® CROSSWORDS™

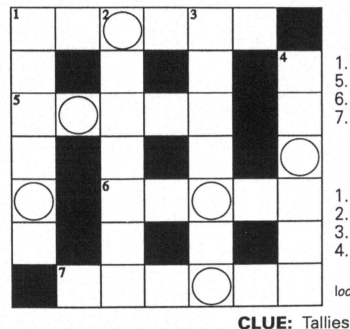

ACROSS

CLUE		ANSWER
1.	Pushed in	E E D D T N
5.	A type of coffee	H A M O C
6.	Sign up	R E E T N
7.	Princess loved by Cupid	H Y S C E P

DOWN

CLUE		ANSWER
1.	Death	S I D M E E
2.	Central point	L U C E N S U
3.	Flexible	S L A E C I T
4.	Origin	R O U S E C

How to play - Complete the crossword puzzle by looking at the clues and unscrambling the answers. When the puzzle is complete, unscramble the circled letters to solve the BONUS.

DOUBLE BONUS

The circled letters can be unscrambled to form two different BONUS answers.

CLUE: Tallies

CLUE: Home to approx. 500,000

JUMBLE CROSSWORDS™

ACROSS

CLUE		ANSWER
1.	Chunk	UTNGEG
5.	Track	ECTAR
6.	Bring together	TINEU
7.	Plant disease	HIBTLG

DOWN

CLUE		ANSWER
1.	Spot	CONEIT
2.	Slight	ARGLADU
3.	Beginning of night	GNIVEEN
4.	Particular time	OTMNME

How to play - Complete the crossword puzzle by looking at the clues and unscrambling the answers. When the puzzle is complete, unscramble the circled letters to solve the BONUS.

DOUBLE BONUS

The circled letters can be unscrambled to form two different BONUS answers.

CLUE: Retaliate

CLUE: Found in Europe

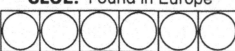

PUZZLE #178

JUMBLE CROSSWORDS™

ACROSS

CLUE	ANSWER
1. Pacific island	HITIAT
5. 6th sign of the zodiac	GVRIO
6. Finely ground meal	ROFUL
7. Customer	NICTLE

DOWN

CLUE	ANSWER
1. Saloon	VTREAN
2. Unhealthful	LHUAFRM
3. Simon and Garfunkel	STOWEOM
4. A type of bird	RPTORA

How to play - Complete the crossword puzzle by looking at the clues and unscrambling the answers. When the puzzle is complete, unscramble the circled letters to solve the BONUS.

CLUE: Item

DOUBLE BONUS

The circled letters can be unscrambled to form two different BONUS answers.

CLUE: A type of performance

#179

JUMBLE CROSSWORDS™

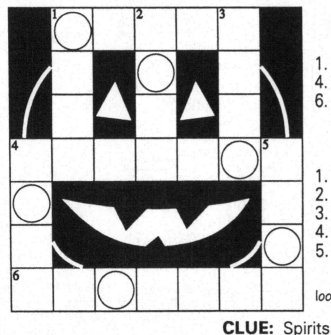

ACROSS

CLUE		ANSWER
1. Costume		TPUEG
4. Competent		PCAAELB
6. Extravagantly generous		OPFRUES

DOWN

CLUE		ANSWER
1. Celebration		LAAG
2. Horn		TAUB
3. Tablet		LPIL
4. Young boy		ACHP
5. Other, different		SELE

How to play - Complete the crossword puzzle by looking at the clues and unscrambling the answers. When the puzzle is complete, unscramble the circled letters to solve the BONUS.

DOUBLE BONUS

The circled letters can be unscrambled to form two different BONUS answers.

CLUE: Spirits

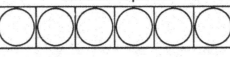

CLUE: Swampy area

PUZZLE

#180

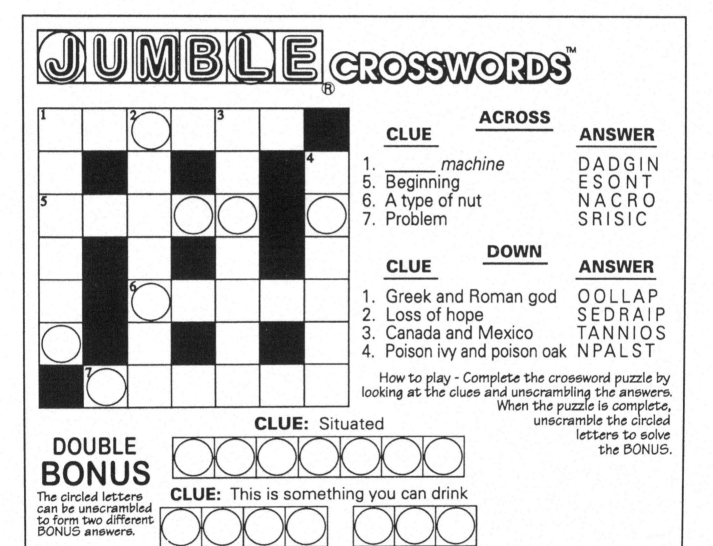

JUMBLE CROSSWORDS™

ACROSS

CLUE	ANSWER
1. _____ machine	DADGIN
5. Beginning	ESONT
6. A type of nut	NACRO
7. Problem	SRISIC

DOWN

CLUE	ANSWER
1. Greek and Roman god	OOLLAP
2. Loss of hope	SEDRAIP
3. Canada and Mexico	TANNIOS
4. Poison ivy and poison oak	NPALST

How to play - Complete the crossword puzzle by looking at the clues and unscrambling the answers. When the puzzle is complete, unscramble the circled letters to solve the BONUS.

DOUBLE BONUS

The circled letters can be unscrambled to form two different BONUS answers.

CLUE: Situated

○○○○○○○

CLUE: This is something you can drink

○○○○ ○○○

183

ANSWERS

1. **Answers:**
   1A—INFORM 5A—SCALE 6A—HAUNT 7A—BROKER
   1D—INSECT 2D—FEATHER 3D—ROEBUCK 4D—SUITOR
   Bonus: A traveler—TOURIST

2. **Answers:**
   1A—PIMPLE 5A—LILAC 6A—STUMP 7A—CAREER
   1D—PULSAR 2D—MELISSA 3D—LECTURE 4D—DIAPER
   Bonus: Confident—ASSURED

3. **Answers:**
   1A—WINTER 5A—NAMES 6A—REACH 7A—PLAYER
   1D—WANTED 2D—NUMERAL 3D—ECSTASY 4D—TETHER
   Bonus: Settled comfortably—NESTLED

4. **Answers:**
   1A—DETACH 5A—SHIED 6A—KNIFE 7A—REPEAL
   1D—DOSAGE 2D—TRICKLE 3D—CODEINE 4D—LINEAL
   Bonus: Yours may need to be given—CONSENT

5. **Answers:**
   1A—ELAPSE 5A—ADAMS 6A—TRIPE 7A—CRINGE
   1D—ENAMEL 2D—ADAPTER 3D—SESSION 4D—DELETE
   Bonus: You are responsible for yours—ACTIONS

6. **Answers:**
   1A—REBATE 5A—FORCE 6A—DEBIT 7A—EMBERS
   1D—RAFFLE 2D—BOREDOM 3D—TREMBLE 4D—CACTUS
   Bonus: Why—BECAUSE

7. **Answers:**
   1A—VULGAR 5A—LIBRA 6A—NANNA 7A—KNOTTY
   1D—VULCAN 2D—LEBANON 3D—AGAINST 4D—SWEATY
   Bonus: A reason to take aim—BOWLING

8. **Answers:**
   1A—ADVICE 5A—BLAND 6A—UNITE 7A—ITCHED
   1D—ALBANY 2D—VIADUCT 3D—CODFISH 4D—THREAD
   Bonus: You might want to fill up with this—UNLEADED

9. **Answers:**
   1A—DECADE 5A—VENOM 6A—UTTER 7A—STODGY
   1D—DIVIDE 2D—CONSULT 3D—DEMOTED 4D—CHERRY
   Bonus: A type of place—SECOND

10. **Answers:**
    1A—GRUBBY 5A—OSAKA 6A—MOLAR 7A—EDISON
    1D—GEORGE 2D—UNARMED 3D—BEATLES 4D—PATRON
    Bonus: You might require this to be safe—PASSAGE

11. **Answers:**
    1A—SHOWER 5A—EATER 6A—OPTIC 7A—DESCRY
    1D—SLEDGE 2D—OUTCOME 3D—ERRATIC 4D—STOCKY
    Bonus: This can brighten your day—DAYLIGHT

12. **Answers:**
    1A—NOTIFY 5A—USAGE 6A—HOKUM 7A—BREEZE
    1D—NAUSEA 2D—TEACHER 3D—FRECKLE 4D—STYMIE
    Bonus: An opening, store or supply—OUTLET

13. **Answers:**
    1A—TRAGIC 5A—ISAAC 6A—ELITE 7A—PRIEST
    1D—TOILET 2D—AMATEUR 3D—INCLINE 4D—POTENT
    Bonus: A type of shock—SURPRISE

14. **Answers:**
    1A—WEIGHT 5A—NIFTY 6A—RHINO 7A—COMEDY
    1D—WINTRY 2D—INFERNO 3D—HAYWIRE 4D—BLOODY
    Bonus: A vacation spot of "Maude" character—FLORIDA

15. **Answers:**
    1A—COUSIN 5A—RURAL 6A—VOCAL 7A—PLATED
    1D—CURFEW 2D—UNRAVEL 3D—ILLICIT 4D—MAILED
    Bonus: Longer play or higher pay—OVERTIME

16. **Answers:**
    1A—ALASKA 5A—SATIN 6A—RUPEE 7A—ADONIS
    1D—ASSUME 2D—ALTERED 3D—KINGPIN 4D—PLIERS
    Bonus: D. J., M. D., P. T. and M. N.—MONKEES

17. **Answers:**
    1A—PUZZLE 5A—NASTY 6A—FLIER 7A—PLAYED
    1D—PENCIL 2D—ZESTFUL 3D—LOYALTY 4D—SACRED
    Bonus: A great misfortune—DISASTER

18. **Answers:**
    1A—CHROME 5A—RECAP 6A—IDIOT 7A—HEIGHT
    1D—CURSOR 2D—RECLINE 3D—MOPPING 4D—SEPTET
    Bonus: A Roman god and a celestial body—NEPTUNE

19. **Answers:**
    1A—RUINED 5A—DRAMA 6A—ISSUE 7A—HERDED
    1D—RODENT 2D—IMAGINE 3D—ELAPSED 4D—BEHEAD
    Bonus: These can be good or bad—HABITS

20. **Answers:**
    1A—PISTON 5A—AWARD 6A—PAPER 7A—PRISON
    1D—PEANUT 2D—SCAMPER 3D—OEDIPUS 4D—OUTRUN
    Bonus: They are older than you—PARENTS

21. **Answers:**
    1A—STRIPE 5A—ITCHY 6A—VOICE 7A—CRISIS
    1D—SOILED 2D—RECOVER 3D—PHYSICS 4D—ACCESS
    Bonus: Of enduring interest—CLASSIC

22. **Answers:**
    1A—ABSORB 5A—PRICE 6A—KNIFE 7A—BRIGHT
    1D—APPEAR 2D—STICKER 3D—REELING 4D—ABSENT
    Bonus: A place with many rooms—HOSPITAL

23. **Answers:**
    1A—SPLASH 5A—NOTES 6A—REIGN 7A—SLINKY
    1D—SENATE 2D—LATERAL 3D—SESSION 4D—MAINLY
    Bonus: Average—NORMAL

24. **Answers:**
    1A—HEALTH 5A—RERUN 6A—ABIDE 7A—PLUNGE
    1D—HERMIT 2D—AIRMAIL 3D—TENSION 4D—CHEESE
    Bonus: This has to do with the middle—CENTRAL

25. **Answers:**
    1A—MAGNUM 5A—STAGE 6A—ONSET 7A—FROLIC
    1D—MISSED 2D—GLAMOUR 3D—UTENSIL 4D—ARCTIC
    Bonus: This can be used when speaking—SARCASM

26. **Answers:**
    1A—SHREWD 5A—RACER 6A—ISAAC 7A—STATUE
    1D—STREET 2D—RECEIPT 3D—WARRANT 4D—MUSCLE
    Bonus: Second largest, sixth farthest—SATURN

27. **Answers:**
    1A—GROOVE 5A—MOTOR 6A—OWNER 7A—ATTAIN
    1D—GEMINI 2D—OUTPOST 3D—VERANDA 4D—NEURON
    Bonus: Yours can be given—OPINION

28. **Answers:**
    1A—SNOOZE 5A—MARIA 6A—MOODY 7A—UNISEX
    1D—SAMPLE 2D—OARSMAN 3D—LARYNX 4D—EXPLORER
    Bonus: An astronaut can be considered one—EXPLORER

29. **Answers:**
    1A—REPLAY 5A—NORTH 6A—OCEAN 7A—PATENT
    1D—RENTAL 2D—PERSONA 3D—ATHLETE 4D—PEANUT
    Bonus: Redford was one in a movie—NATURAL

30. **Answers:**
    1A—NEARBY 5A—WAVES 6A—NIECE 7A—MESHED
    1D—NEWARK 2D—ADVANCE 3D—BESEECH 4D—ATTEND
    Bonus: You can find tape in one—CASSETTE

31. **Answers:**
    1A—UNPACK 5A—SINUS 6A—ADULT 7A—FLEECE
    1D—UNSAFE 2D—PINBALL 3D—COSTUME 4D—BATTLE
    Bonus: A type of home—CASTLE

32. **Answers:**
    1A—PAGODA 5A—INNER 6A—HAVEN 7A—STODGY
    1D—PRINCE 2D—GUNSHOT 3D—DERIVED 4D—TRENDY
    Bonus: "An Elvis" can be a type of this—SIGHTING

33. **Answers:**
    1A—DUFFER 5A—PAGER 6A—ELITE 7A—STORMY
    1D—DEPART 2D—FIGMENT 3D—EARLIER 4D—JEREMY
    Bonus: Known for being the largest—JUPITER

34. **Answers:**
    1A—PACIFY 5A—PEACE 6A—LEILA 7A—ENIGMA
    1D—POPPED 2D—CHAPLIN 3D—FLEEING 4D—SONATA
    Bonus: An event that may have serious consequences—INCIDENT

35. **Answers:**
    1A—RETINA 5A—SOBER 6A—OZONE 7A—ODESSA
    1D—RUSSIA 2D—TABLOID 3D—NERVOUS 4D—CINEMA
    Bonus: These are handpowered—SCISSORS

36. **Answers:**
    1A—ORANGE 5A—TUNER 6A—SLICE 7A—FATHER
    1D—OUTFIT 2D—AMNESIA 3D—GARNISH 4D—LINEAR
    Bonus: Written words can be this—FICTION

37. **Answers:**
1A—REVOKE 5A—SIREN 6A—OBESE 7A—STATUS
1D—RUSTIC 2D—VERMONT 3D—KINDEST 4D—RECESS
Bonus: A naturally dark place—CAVERN

38. **Answers:**
1A—RAFFLE 5A—VISTA 6A—IMAGE 7A—INFECT
1D—REVERT 2D—FASHION 3D—LEAKAGE 4D—ACCENT
Bonus: If this is bad, you might be late—TRAFFIC

39. **Answers:**
1A—VOLUME 5A—RHINE 6A—UNIFY 7A—WEDGED
1D—VERSUS 2D—LEISURE 3D—MEETING 4D—OBEYED
Bonus: A family of actors (L. B., B. B. and J. B.)—BRIDGES

40. **Answers:**
1A—EXPAND 5A—ELBOW 6A—INEPT 7A—THREAD
1D—EYELID 2D—PUBLISH 3D—NOWHERE 4D—POSTED
Bonus: A film about Michael Dorsey as Dorothy Michaels—
TOOTSIE

41. **Answers:**
1A—HUDSON 5A—RUSTY 6A—UNPIN 7A—LESSON
1D—HURRAH 2D—DISPUTE 3D—OLYMPUS 4D—CANNON
Bonus: Sean Connery is this—SCOTTISH

42. **Answers:**
1A—ABRUPT 5A—RIFLE 6A—SMELL 7A—OLDEST
1D—ACROSS 2D—REFUSAL 3D—PRECEDE 4D—CHALET
Bonus: You may be this now—CLUELESS

43. **Answers:**
1A—FIGURE 5A—ARENA 6A—LATIN 7A—ENTREE
1D—FRANCE 2D—GREMLIN 3D—ROASTER 4D—CHANCE
Bonus: You can make one, or carry some—CHANGE

44. **Answers:**
1A—ROBUST 5A—SALON 6A—VIBES 7A—HANGAR
1D—RUSHED 2D—BOLIVIA 3D—SANDBAG 4D—SENSOR
Bonus: This can come before up, water or tall—STANDING

45. **Answers:**
1A—KARATE 5A—NUDGE 6A—ISSUE 7A—CHANGE
1D—KANSAS 2D—REDDISH 3D—TREASON 4D—ALLEGE
Bonus: A root used in food and drink preparation—GINGER

46. **Answers:**
1A—MEDIUM 5A—RISER 6A—ELVES 7A—STALIN
1D—MORROW 2D—DESCENT 3D—UNRAVEL 4D—CHOSEN
Bonus: You might have to look down to see this word—WELCOME

47. **Answers:**
1A—MOHAWK 5A—MICRO 6A—LIGHT 7A—CRAYON
1D—MEMORY 2D—HECKLER 3D—WRONGLY 4D—FASTEN
Bonus: A type of zone or level—COMFORT

48. **Answers:**
1A—ALWAYS 5A—CRIMP 6A—TWIST 7A—ENIGMA
1D—ARCHIE 2D—WRITTEN 3D—YAPPING 4D—AGATHA
Bonus: This was basic to Michael and Sharon—INSTINCT

49. **Answers:**
1A—RABBIT 5A—STERN 6A—INNER 7A—CHOSEN
1D—RESORT 2D—BLEMISH 3D—INNINGS 4D—MICRON
Bonus: Well-known, of great importance—HISTORIC

50. **Answers:**
1A—STREAK 5A—PAPER 6A—LIVEN 7A—DEPLOY
1D—SEPTIC 2D—REPULSE 3D—ARRIVAL 4D—MAINLY
Bonus: Guests can be considered this—COMPANY

51. **Answers:**
1A—SHABBY 5A—MIAMI 6A—ADAGE 7A—LAUNCH
1D—SAMPLE 2D—ALABAMA 3D—BRITAIN 4D—SPEECH
Bonus: C. K.'s other name—SUPERMAN

52. **Answers:**
1A—SELECT 5A—LIVES 6A—BLIND 7A—HERNIA
1D—SALOON 2D—LOVABLE 3D—CUSHION 4D—SANDRA
Bonus: A show of approval—OVATION

53. **Answers:**
1A—FACADE 5A—ELUDE 6A—ATLAS 7A—VENDOR
1D—FLETCH 2D—COURAGE 3D—DUELLED 4D—KISSER
Bonus: A group of people from the 70s—VILLAGE

54. **Answers:**
1A—REPEAT 5A—CHESS 6A—UNRIG 7A—LEGACY
1D—RECALL 2D—PRESUME 3D—AUSTRIA 4D—SMUGLY
Bonus: A famous first's first name—HILLARY

55. **Answers:**
1A—ADRIFT 5A—SUPER 6A—IRISH 7A—ATTEST
1D—ASSIGN 2D—REPRINT 3D—FORGIVE 4D—UPSHOT
Bonus: This can be a small book—PASSPORT

56. **Answers:**
1A—STROBE 5A—IGLOO 6A—PADRE 7A—HEARSE
1D—SPINAL 2D—RELAPSE 3D—BROADER 4D—SCHEME
Bonus: Found in a bathroom; or a W. B. movie from 1975—
SHAMPOO

57. **Answers:**
1A—CHARGE 5A—UPSET 6A—NEIGH 7A—RECKON
1D—CRUISE 2D—ABSENCE 3D—GATWICK 4D—PYTHON
Bonus: Void, zero or insignificant—NOTHING

58. **Answers:**
1A—FLASHY 5A—ZEBRA 6A—ETHEL 7A—STORMY
1D—FIZZLE 2D—AMBIENT 3D—HEATHER 4D—WOOLLY
Bonus: More common the farther north or south you go—
SNOWFALL

59. **Answers:**
1A—METRIC 5A—TENSE 6A—RUINS 7A—AMENDS
1D—MOTHER 2D—TANTRUM 3D—IBERIAN 4D—CRISIS
Bonus: Mona hangs here—MUSEUM

60. **Answers:**
1A—REMEDY 5A—PIGGY 6A—CHORD 7A—SLOGAN
1D—RAPTOR 2D—MAGICAL 3D—DAYLONG 4D—BURDEN
Bonus: This performer's name might escape you—HOUDINI

61. **Answers:**
1A—POLICE 5A—TORSO 6A—HYENA 7A—EDITOR
1D—PETITE 2D—LURCHED 3D—COOLEST 4D—ECLAIR
Bonus: A reason to get the scissors—COUPON

62. **Answers:**
1A—MISTER 5A—TALES 6A—REEDS 7A—KERNEL
1D—MOTIVE 2D—SPLURGE 3D—EASTERN 4D—CHISEL
Bonus: Permission—LICENSE

63. **Answers:**
1A—REFORM 5A—LICKS 6A—USERS 7A—BLITHE
1D—ROLLED 2D—FACTUAL 3D—RESPECT 4D—JESSIE
Bonus: The answer is this—JUMBLED

64. **Answers:**
1A—PRAGUE 5A—LADEN 6A—TIMER 7A—GRADES
1D—POLICY 2D—AUDITOR 3D—UNNAMED 4D—CHORUS
Bonus: George's last or Ford's first—HARRISON

65. **Answers:**
1A—SPLASH 5A—ORGAN 6A—COUNT 7A—GLANCE
1D—SPONGE 2D—LOGICAL 3D—SUNBURN 4D—MYRTLE
Bonus: Strength—COURAGE

66. **Answers:**
1A—EUROPE 5A—EASED 6A—RULER 7A—LEADED
1D—ELEVEN 2D—RESERVE 3D—PEDDLED 4D—JARRED
Bonus: A country, river or athlete—JORDAN

67. **Answers:**
1A—PRESTO 5A—ARENA 6A—UNION 7A—WEIGHT
1D—PEAKED 2D—EXECUTE 3D—TRADING 4D—BONNET
Bonus: A + B + C can equal one—NETWORK

68. **Answers:**
1A—SQUISH 5A—OLDER 6A—RATED 7A—GOPHER
1D—SLOPPY 2D—UNDERGO 3D—STRETCH 4D—WONDER
Bonus: Bacteria helps create this—YOGURT

69. **Answers:**
1A—UPTOWN 5A—PLANT 6A—FRAIL 7A—FLUENT
1D—UMPIRE 2D—TEARFUL 3D—WATTAGE 4D—BULLET
Bonus: This point changes with altitude—BOILING

70. **Answers:**
1A—SNEEZE 5A—RATIO 6A—NAILS 7A—STIGMA
1D—SCRIPT 2D—EXTINCT 3D—ZOOMING 4D—MARSHA
Bonus: A James that played a "Jim"—GARNER

71. **Answers:**
1A—ZEPHYR 5A—RHODA 6A—IONIC 7A—SEEDED
1D—ZURICH 2D—PROVIDED 3D—YEARNED 4D—TRACED
Bonus: A way to get from one point to another using your feet—
TRAIPSE

72. **Answers:**
1A—VENICE 5A—LATER 6A—BRUTE 7A—SEXTET
1D—VALLEY 2D—NOTABLE 3D—CIRCUIT 4D—WISEST
Bonus: This is always a woman—WAITRESS

73. **Answers:**
1A—SCREAM 5A—LIFTS 6A—SAUCE 7A—BLOTCH
1D—SPLICE 2D—REFUSAL 3D—ASSAULT 4D—JOSEPH
Bonus: You might find one on a table—COASTER

74. **Answers:**
1A—SHINER 5A—INPUT 6A—ORATE 7A—PEANUT
1D—SWITCH 2D—IMPLODE 3D—ENTRAIN 4D—SELECT
Bonus: This can be high, low or intense—PRESSURE

75. **Answers:**
1A—NIBBLE 5A—BAMBI 6A—STUNG 7A—ODDEST
1D—NOBODY 2D—BEMUSED 3D—LEISURE 4D—PLIGHT
Bonus: H. S. M. S., B. S., L. S. and M. S.—SIMPSONS

76. **Answers:**
1A—PILLAR 5A—REACT 6A—HYENA 7A—PRISON
1D—PARKED 2D—LEATHER 3D—ACTRESS 4D—STRAIN
Bonus: You might find one at the end of a wire—SPEAKER

77. **Answers:**
1A—SLIGHT 5A—ANNUL 6A—RAILS 7A—ADAGIO
1D—SHAMED 2D—IGNORED 3D—HELPING 4D—FIASCO
Bonus: A beginning that feels like an ending—MIDNIGHT

78. **Answers:**
1A—POETIC 5A—LOUIS 6A—DRIFT 7A—ORDEAL
1D—PALACE 2D—ECUADOR 3D—INSPIRE 4D—MENTAL
Bonus: If you don't take this, you might lose it—CONTROL

79. **Answers:**
1A—MORALE 5A—TANGY 6A—LILAC 7A—STAYED
1D—MATURE 2D—RINGLET 3D—LOYALLY 4D—VOICED
Bonus: This debuted in January of 1953—CORVETTE

80. **Answers:**
1A—CINEMA 5A—TOWED 6A—OMAHA 7A—STREAK
1D—CATTLE 2D—NEWPORT 3D—MEDIATE 4D—UNMASK
Bonus: Handle—STOMACH

81. **Answers:**
1A—ERRANT 5A—AIDED 6A—ABIDE 7A—STAGED
1D—ELAPSE 2D—RADIANT 3D—NODDING 4D—FRIEND
Bonus: Related to three w's—INTERNET

82. **Answers:**
1A—LONDON 5A—EASEL 6A—RIGID 7A—ELUDED
1D—LEEWAY 2D—NOSTRIL 3D—OBLIGED 4D—BONDED
Bonus: You can see in this manner—DOUBLE

83. **Answers:**
1A—ACCEPT 5A—RURAL 6A—MOUTH 7A—SCREWY
1D—ARRIVE 2D—CERAMIC 3D—POLLUTE 4D—EIGHTY
Bonus: Who cares?—WHATEVER

84. **Answers:**
1A—UNSAFE 5A—TEASE 6A—LODGE 7A—SWAMPY
1D—UPTURN 2D—SHALLOW 3D—FREEDOM 4D—BAKERY
Bonus: One corner of a triangle—BERMUDA

85. **Answers:**
1A—VERBAL 5A—YEMEN 6A—RATED 7A—METEOR
1D—VOYAGE 2D—REMORSE 3D—ANNETTE 4D—CONDOR
Bonus: This chain can be made of people—COMMAND

86. **Answers:**
1A—AMOEBA 5A—NOTED 6A—BRICK 7A—CREEPY
1D—ARNOLD 2D—OCTOBER 3D—BEDTIME 4D—SICKLY
Bonus: Players use bats when playing this—CRICKET

87. **Answers:**
1A—ZURICH 5A—GAPED 6A—IRISH 7A—METHOD
1D—ZIGZAG 2D—REPTILE 3D—CODFISH 4D—BASHED
Bonus: An idea can be considered this—BRIGHT

88. **Answers:**
1A—SERVED 5A—MAFIA 6A—SATIN 7A—PLAYER
1D—SAMPLE 2D—REFUSAL 3D—EXACTLY 4D—SHINER
Bonus: An exam—PHYSICAL

89. **Answers:**
1A—REMEDY 5A—MERGE 6A—ICING 7A—SINGLE
1D—REMAIN 2D—MARTINI 3D—DIETING 4D—PLAGUE
Bonus: An assertion, basis for an argument—PREMISE

90. **Answers:**
1A—SAVAGE 5A—LAYER 6A—GREED 7A—CRATER
1D—SPLINT 2D—VOYAGER 3D—GARMENT 4D—BORDER
Bonus: An undesirable outcome—DEBACLE

91. **Answers:**
1A—TENNIS 5A—AISLE 6A—ROADS 7A—GLIDER
1D—THAWED 2D—NOSTRIL 3D—ICELAND 4D—PASSER
Bonus: Last name of a famous actor, singer and driver—STEWART

92. **Answers:**
1A—SPRAIN 5A—REFIT 6A—ERUPT 7A—SHREWD
1D—SURELY 2D—REFRESH 3D—INTRUDE 4D—DENTED
Bonus: Something might appear this way—SUDDENLY

93. **Answers:**
1A—STICKY 5A—TAPER 6A—ATTIC 7A—STONED
1D—SATIRE 2D—IMPLANT 3D—KERATIN 4D—VISCID
Bonus: A word before school, life or matter—PRIVATE

94. **Answers:**
1A—TENANT 5A—IDAHO 6A—ELLIS 7A—STASIS
1D—TWITCH 2D—NEAREST 3D—NOODLES 4D—CENSUS
Bonus: You might put one in a bag—SANDWICH

95. **Answers:**
1A—FOLLOW 5A—RUMBA 6A—OLIVE 7A—ENIGMA
1D—FERRIS 2D—LAMPOON 3D—ORATING 4D—ATHENA
Bonus: A type of fee—POSTAGE

96. **Answers:**
1A—SCRIPT 5A—OWNED 6A—WRONG 7A—FLAKED
1D—STORMY 2D—RENEWAL 3D—PADLOCK 4D—HOGGED
Bonus: You might go to jail if you play this—MONOPOLY

97. **Answers:**
1A—VISUAL 5A—VENUS 6A—EMEND 7A—GEYSER
1D—VIVIAN 2D—SINCERE 3D—ABSCESS 4D—KINDER
Bonus: This can cause severe pain—MIGRAINE

98. **Answers:**
1A—NEARBY 5A—GARTH 6A—AIMED 7A—STRATA
1D—NUGGET 2D—ABREAST 3D—BOHEMIA 4D—TUNDRA
Bonus: A word before control or after storm—DAMAGE

99. **Answers:**
1A—MENACE 5A—TITAN 6A—OXIDE 7A—SKINNY
1D—MUTINY 2D—NETWORK 3D—CONSIGN 4D—NICELY
Bonus: You may be prone to put this after natural—TENDENCY

100. **Answers:**
1A—NATURE 5A—TRIPE 6A—EXIST 7A—STIGMA
1D—NOTION 2D—TRIDENT 3D—REELING 4D—MARTHA
Bonus: A broken one may cause problems—PROMISE

101. **Answers:**
1A—SLATED 5A—NIGHT 6A—BRUCE 7A—CAREEN
1D—SUNDAE 2D—ALGEBRA 3D—ENTHUSE 4D—ASTERN
Bonus: If a number is this, it will be harder to find—UNLISTED

102. **Answers:**
1A—TARIFF 5A—GOFER 6A—ELITE 7A—CHEERS
1D—TUGGED 2D—REFRESH 3D—FERTILE 4D—ABBESS
Bonus: It's hard to get out of this once you're in it—TROUBLE

103. **Answers:**
1A—PLUNGE 5A—NYLON 6A—ASIAN 7A—THREAT
1D—PENCIL 2D—UNLEASH 3D—GUNFIRE 4D—SONNET
Bonus: Low ones may result in a cancellation—RATINGS

104. **Answers:**
1A—ARCHIE 5A—RAINY 6A—KILLS 7A—FENCED
1D—ARROWS 2D—CRINKLE 3D—IDYLLIC 4D—CLOSED
Bonus: A 7th and a 1st together equals one—WEEKEND

105. **Answers:**
1A—CRAFTY 5A—DAVID 6A—SILVA 7A—OSPREY
1D—CADGER 2D—ADVISES 3D—TODDLER 4D—ROTARY
Bonus: You may have to keep yours low—PROFILE

106. **Answers:**
1A—INSIDE 5A—JULIA 6A—REEFS 7A—BESTED
1D—INJURY 2D—SPLURGE 3D—DEAREST 4D—HOUSED
Bonus: A reason to be happy—BIRTHDAY

107. **Answers:**
1A—MUMBLE 5A—YOURS 6A—IRONY 7A—FENDER
1D—MAYHEM 2D—MAURICE 3D—LASSOED 4D—LAWYER
Bonus: Independence—FREEDOM

108. **Answers:**
1A—ABRUPT 5A—SOFIA 6A—ALPHA 7A—STENCH
1D—ASSIST 2D—REFRACT 3D—PLAYPEN 4D—DETACH
Bonus: One side of this is often a picture—POSTCARD

109. **Answers:**
1A—CHOOSE 5A—MATCH 6A—OILED 7A—DEBRIS
1D—COMMON 2D—OUTCOME 3D—SCHOLAR 4D—EXODUS
Bonus: This TV character was quite a character—COLUMBO

110. **Answers:**
1A—SUPERB 5A—OVOID 6A—USAGE 7A—STATUS
1D—SLOWLY 2D—PRODUCT 3D—RADIANT 4D—UNLESS
Bonus: "Charlie's" last name—TOWNSEND

111. **Answers:**
1A—CREATE 5A—YARDS 6A—ELLIS 7A—STUDIO
1D—CRYING 2D—EARNEST 3D—TUSSLED 4D—FIASCO
Bonus: G. S. and R. E. to the movie business—CRITICS

186

112. **Answers:**
1A—WRENCH 5A—ICTUS 6A—ALICE 7A—STOGIE
1D—WEIGHT 2D—EXTRACT 3D—CASTING 4D—IMPEDE
Bonus: Yours may vary—MILEAGE

113. **Answers:**
1A—PARODY 5A—NEVER 6A—OMAHA 7A—MILTON
1D—PANDAS 2D—RAVIOLI 3D—DORMANT 4D—DOMAIN
Bonus: Similar looking but different, like dash and dash—HOMONYMS

114. **Answers:**
1A—PERISH 5A—CLAMS 6A—THEME 7A—PROTON
1D—PACINO 2D—REACTOR 3D—SUSPECT 4D—SCREEN
Bonus: "Cheers," "All in the Family," "Happy Days"—SITCOMS

115. **Answers:**
1A—VIENNA 5A—LAPIN 6A—OFTEN 7A—DEEPLY
1D—VALUED 2D—EXPLORE 3D—NONSTOP 4D—SHANTY
Bonus: Found along the side of a road—HYDRANT

116. **Answers:**
1A—BOSTON 5A—APART 6A—INGOT 7A—MINNOW
1D—BRAIDS 2D—SWAHILI 3D—OCTAGON 4D—BESTOW
Bonus: You are always waiting for this—TOMORROW

117. **Answers:**
1A—PYTHON 5A—ADAGE 6A—POINT 7A—BEAKER
1D—PLAINS 2D—TRAMPLE 3D—OBELISK 4D—MENTOR
Bonus: A fictional warrior race—KLINGON

118. **Answers:**
1A—REAPER 5A—LEGOS 6A—AGNES 7A—ASCEND
1D—RELIEF 2D—AFGHANS 3D—ESSENCE 4D—PHASED
Bonus: "Maude" and "Laverne and Shirley"—SPINOFFS

119. **Answers:**
1A—FOSSIL 5A—TEASE 6A—GATES 7A—CREAMY
1D—FUTURE 2D—STAGGER 3D—INERTIA 4D—CRISPY
Bonus: A crossword puzzle is one—PASTIME

120. **Answers:**
1A—SCULPT 5A—LOUSY 6A—USERS 7A—PLATES
1D—SALTED 2D—UNUSUAL 3D—PAYMENT 4D—THESIS
Bonus: Home to the brothers Crane—SEATTLE

121. **Answers:**
1A—VANISH 5A—NAIVE 6A—HEAVE 7A—WRITES
1D—VENICE 2D—NEITHER 3D—STEWART 4D—RECESS
Bonus: A tennis first or second—SERVICE

122. **Answers:**
1A—LOCUST 5A—TRACY 6A—CLARK 7A—PLEDGE
1D—LITTLE 2D—CHANCEL 3D—SKYWARD 4D—PICKLE
Bonus: This person played this puzzle before you did—EDITOR

123. **Answers:**
1A—SATURN 5A—ILIAD 6A—KICKS 7A—STOLEN
1D—SMILED 2D—THICKET 3D—RADICAL 4D—REASON
Bonus: After George or Linda, or before Bermuda—HAMILTON

124. **Answers:**
1A—GLOBAL 5A—ACTOR 6A—ITCHY 7A—KETTLE
1D—GOALIE 2D—OUTLINE 3D—APRICOT 4D—ENZYME
Bonus: A bank service that is sometimes free—CHECKING

125. **Answers:**
1A—DEFECT 5A—PROOF 6A—IRISH 7A—CAESAR
1D—DAPPER 2D—FLORIDA 3D—COFFINS 4D—GATHER
Bonus: A very small country—ANDORRA

126. **Answers:**
1A—CRUMBS 5A—ALERT 6A—RAISE 7A—SHAGGY
1D—CHANGE 2D—UNEARTH 3D—BATHING 4D—NAMELY
Bonus: A sea creature or a car—STINGRAY

127. **Answers:**
1A—CARAFE 5A—WAVES 6A—LOUIS 7A—DETECT
1D—COWBOY 2D—REVOLVE 3D—FISSURE 4D—CLOSET
Bonus: This works like a scale—SEESAW

128. **Answers:**
1A—ENCORE 5A—TURNS 6A—ALERT 7A—ANGLED
1D—EITHER 2D—CERTAIN 3D—RUSSELL 4D—ROOTED
Bonus: This group is sometimes famous for its leader—ORCHESTRA

129. **Answers:**
1A—CASINO 5A—SLUNG 6A—ARENA 7A—BETTER
1D—CASTLE 2D—SAUSAGE 3D—NEGLECT 4D—REPAIR
Bonus: "If x = 5 and y = 2, then x · y = 3," for example—ALGEBRA

130. **Answers:**
1A—MAGNET 5A—SCRAP 6A—LUNAR 7A—CADETS
1D—MISSED 2D—GORILLA 3D—EXPANSE 4D—CITRUS
Bonus: One reason to wear a hat and glasses—DISGUISE

131. **Answers:**
1A—CATCHY 5A—MACAW 6A—FAVOR 7A—CLERIC
1D—COMBAT 2D—TACTFUL 3D—HOWEVER 4D—NITRIC
Bonus: "(3 + 8 - 1 + 2) x 2 + 1 = 36," for example—INCORRECT

132. **Answers:**
1A—WARREN 5A—TIGER 6A—ORGAN 7A—SPIDER
1D—WITHER 2D—REGROUP 3D—ENRAGED 4D—TURNER
Bonus: Elizabeth and Victoria, and Edward and George?—TWO PAIR (2 QUEENS AND 2 KINGS)

133. **Answers:**
1A—EYELET 5A—EIGHT 6A—ECLAT 7A—EDWARD
1D—EMERGE 2D—EGGHEAD 3D—ESTELLA 4D—ELATED
Bonus: You don't know how hard it was to make all the answers—START WITH "E"

134. **Answers:**
1A—PLENTY 5A—IRENE 6A—ELMER 7A—STASIS
1D—PRINCE 2D—EVEREST 3D—THERMOS 4D—TAURUS
Bonus: Plans—ITINERARY

135. **Answers:**
1A—FATHOM 5A—LOUIS 6A—TRUMP 7A—DECENT
1D—FILTER 2D—TRUSTEE 3D—OBSCURE 4D—PULPIT
Bonus: Exact—SPECIFIC

136. **Answers:**
1A—HANNAH 5A—CLUED 6A—REEVE 7A—UNUSED
1D—HECKLE 2D—NEUTRON 3D—ADDRESS 4D—LEGEND
Bonus: "I bet you can't finish this puzzle without looking at the answers for help"—CHALLENGE

137. **Answers:**
1A—BOVINE 5A—MOLAR 6A—ABOUT 7A—STAKES
1D—BUMPED 2D—VALIANT 3D—NORFOLK 4D—MANTIS
Bonus: "Find the value of 'X' if A = 1, B = 2 and Y = 3, in the formula (A + Y) - (B + Z) = X," for example—IMPOSSIBLE

138. **Answers:**
1A—ACROSS 5A—TEASE 6A—TIRED 7A—TRADED
1D—ANTHEM 2D—REACTOR 3D—SHEARED 4D—LANDED
Bonus: A reason to turn around—DEAD END

139. **Answers:**
1A—BAKERY 5A—CHILD 6A—GRASS 7A—UNREAL
1D—BICKER 2D—KLINGON 3D—RADIATE 4D—TASSEL
Bonus: Its length is equivalent to 0.9144 of a meter—YARDSTICK

140. **Answers:**
1A—LARGER 5A—DRAMA 6A—TYLER 7A—FRIDAY
1D—LEDGER 2D—REACTOR 3D—ENABLED 4D—STORMY
Bonus: DOODLE

141. **Answers:**
1A—MUFFIN 5A—STOUT 6A—INSURE 7A—LAMENT
1D—MISTER 2D—FLORIDA 3D—INTRUDE 4D—SELECT
Bonus: Jerry, Elaine, and George, but not Kramer, on Seinfeld—FIRST NAMES

142. **Answers:**
1A—AFRICA 5A—BASIS 6A—EXILE 7A—STANCE
1D—ALBANY 2D—RESPECT 3D—CASPIAN 4D—COHERE
Bonus: Grisham's "The Client"—FICTION

143. **Answers:**
1A—SCHEME 5A—SOLVE 6A—GATED 7A—ANGOLA
1D—SYSTEM 2D—HALOGEN 3D—MAESTRO 4D—SANDRA
Bonus: A source for data, information, facts, etc.—ALMANAC

144. **Answers:**
1A—FUTURE 5A—WENDT 6A—INNER 7A—INLAND
1D—FEWEST 2D—TENSION 3D—ROTUNDA 4D—SCORED
Bonus: Literature classification—NONFICTION

145. **Answers:**
1A—MISHAP 5A—BUMPS 6A—OILED 7A—GENEVA
1D—MOBILE 2D—SOMEONE 3D—ABSOLVE 4D—TUNDRA
Bonus: Abbott and Costello—LAST NAMES

146. **Answers:**
1A—STRING 5A—ALONG 6A—TEENS 7A—CRATER
1D—SPARSE 2D—ROOSTER 3D—NEGLECT 4D—CURSOR
Bonus: Found in a Jumble puzzle—CIRCLES

147. **Answers:**
1A—TATTLE 5A—TUDOR 6A—OTHER 7A—SEEDED
1D—TITLES 2D—TADPOLE 3D—LURCHED 4D—SEARED
Bonus: Columbia and Atlantis—(SPACE) SHUTTLES

148. Answers:
1A—PROMPT 5A—MOTEL 6A—INGOT 7A—TENNIS
1D—PUMMEL 2D—OUTLINE 3D—POLYGON 4D—CACTUS
Bonus: Microsoft and IBM—COMPANIES

149. Answers:
1A—TARSUS 5A—RUMMY 6A—ARSON 7A—PERSON
1D—TURRET 2D—RUMMAGE 3D—ULYSSES 4D—CANNON
Bonus: "Unit"—APARTMENT

150. Answers:
1A—WALLOP 5A—ATTIC 6A—UNARM 7A—WEEDED
1D—WEAPON 2D—LETTUCE 3D—ORCHARD 4D—FORMED
Bonus: This puzzle has all _____ _____ clues—TWO WORD

151. Answers:
1A—OTTAWA 5A—DUBAI 6A—LAPSE 7A—BRIDGE
1D—ODDITY 2D—TUBULAR 3D—WHIPPED 4D—GREENE
Bonus: Plan—BLUEPRINT

152. Answers:
1A—SANDRA 5A—PRINT 6A—HATED 7A—GRADED
1D—SIPHON 2D—NEITHER 3D—ROTATED 4D—GUIDED
Bonus: A country—INDONESIA

153. Answers:
1A—COUNTY 5A—MIAMI 6A—ATOLL 7A—MEXICO
1D—COMETS 2D—UNAWARE 3D—TRIPOLI 4D—APOLLO
Bonus: Indonesia, Indiana and Baltimore—LOCATIONS

154. Answers:
1A—APPEAL 5A—CUBIC 6A—ICING 7A—SHREWD
1D—ACCENT 2D—PUBLISH 3D—ASCRIBE 4D—NAGGED
Bonus: A U.S. state—INDIANA

155. Answers:
1A—REMAND 5A—RELIC 6A—ADEPT 7A—SEANCE
1D—RARITY 2D—MILEAGE 3D—NUCLEON 4D—GOATEE
Bonus: This puzzle was much harder than yesterday's puzzle—
COMPARISON

156. Answers:
1A—MATTER 5A—CRETE 6A—RANGE 7A—SMARTS
1D—MICKEY 2D—THEOREM 3D—ELEANOR 4D—BICEPS
Bonus: A city—BALTIMORE

157. Answers:
1A—DUCKED 5A—SNAFU 6A—TITAN 7A—BRIDGE
1D—DESERT 2D—CHATTER 3D—EQUATED 4D—SPONGE
Bonus: Beginning—SQUARE ONE

158. Answers:
1A—FLAUNT 5A—IDIOM 6A—BASED 7A—VERSUS
1D—FRIGHT 2D—AMIABLE 3D—NEMESIS 4D—SPADES
Bonus: Current—UP-TO-DATE

159. Answers:
1A—OTTAWA 5A—RAISE 6A—UTTER 7A—DEFEND
1D—ONRUSH 2D—TRIBUTE 3D—WRESTLE 4D—CONRAD
Bonus: In need of money—DOWN-AND-OUT

160. Answers:
1A—UNSAFE 5A—STAGE 6A—PAGED 7A—POTTER
1D—UNSAID 2D—SHAMPOO 3D—FREIGHT 4D—LENDER
Bonus: Fewer than 50% of the population can make this claim—
LEFT-HANDED

161. Answers:
1A—HARVEY 5A—RESET 6A—FLINT 7A—ALLEGE
1D—HORNET 2D—RESTFUL 3D—ENTWINE 4D—BATTLE
Bonus: Precedence—RIGHT-OF-WAY

162. Answers:
1A—SNEAKY 5A—ALLEN 6A—OPENS 7A—METHOD
1D—SEARED 2D—EPISODE 3D—KENNETH 4D—CEASED
Bonus: Models—PATTERNS

163. Answers:
1A—BECOME 5A—USUAL 6A—PLANE 7A—STODGY
1D—BRUISE 2D—CRUMPET 3D—MALLARD 4D—LIVELY
Bonus: "I love making these puzzles," for example—CURSIVE

164. Answers:
1A—IGUANA 5A—CHEST 6A—RACER 7A—SHADES
1D—INCITE 2D—UNEARTH 3D—NOTICED 4D—BLURBS
Bonus: Certain—IN THE BAG

165. Answers:
1A—NOTION 5A—SHAPE 6A—NEARS 7A—GRILLS
1D—NESTLE 2D—TRAINER 3D—OVERALL 4D—CENSUS
Double Bonus: Hurrying—HUSTLING
The result of a certain nuclear reaction—SUNLIGHT

166. Answers:
1A—GADGET 5A—FACET 6A—IMAGE 7A—BELTED
1D—GIFTED 2D—DECEIVE 3D—ENTRANT 4D—INDEED
Double Bonus: Produce—GENERATE
You may have already been one—TEENAGER

167. Answers:
1A—REPORT 5A—PANDA 6A—CAMEO 7A—NEWTON
1D—REPELS 2D—PANACHE 3D—READMIT 4D—SALOON
Double Bonus: 1, 5, 6 or 7—ACROSS
An annual event—OSCARS

168. Answers:
1A—GALORE 5A—TIGHT 6A—BRING 7A—HECKLE
1D—GOTTEN 2D—LEGIBLE 3D—RETHINK 4D—DANGLE
Double Bonus: Mystery person's status—INCOGNITO
Understanding—COGNITION

169. Answers:
1A—SOCIAL 5A—SOUND 6A—TEMPO 7A—SYDNEY
1D—SISTER 2D—COUNTRY 3D—ABDOMEN 4D—GLOOMY
Double Bonus: Inessential—NEEDLESS
Reduced—LESSENED

170. Answers:
1A—SEARCH 5A—RIDER 6A—BLIND 7A—REDEEM
1D—SURELY 2D—AUDIBLE 3D—CURSIVE 4D—TANDEM
Double Bonus: Inconvenient—UNTIMELY
Insignificant—MINUTELY

171. Answers:
1A—GLOSSY 5A—MOODY 6A—SKIED 7A—AMOEBA
1D—GAMBIT 2D—OPOSSUM 3D—SKYLINE 4D—TUNDRA
Double Bonus: 2nd of 7, or 1st of five—MONDAY
Energetic individual—DYNAMO

172. Answers:
1A—INCOME 5A—FIRST 6A—IVORY 7A—CHOKED
1D—INFANT 2D—CORNISH 3D—MATLOCK 4D—SWAYED
Double Bonus: Pistols, for example—SIDEARMS
Incorrectly interprets—MISREADS

173. Answers:
1A—SALIVA 5A—TIDAL 6A—IMAGE 7A—AGREED
1D—SETTLE 2D—LODGING 3D—VOLTAGE 4D—ASCEND
Double Bonus: Saves—SALVAGES
A city—LAS VEGAS

174. Answers:
1A—CUTTER 5A—DODGE 6A—OMAHA 7A—HEATER
1D—CUDDLE 2D—TADPOLE 3D—ELEGANT 4D—AFFAIR
Double Bonus: Your bank might be yours—CREDITOR
Stone, for example—DIRECTOR

175. Answers:
1A—RESUME 5A—AMONG 6A—EXCEL 7A—STYLUS
1D—ROARED 2D—SLOWEST 3D—MAGICAL 4D—DALLAS
Double Bonus: Flows—STREAMS
Virtuous—MASTERS

176. Answers:
1A—DENTED 5A—MOCHA 6A—ENTER 7A—PSYCHE
1D—DEMISE 2D—NUCLEUS 3D—ELASTIC 4D—SOURCE
Double Bonus: Tallies—COUNTS
Home to approx. 500,000—TUCSON

177. Answers:
1A—NUGGET 5A—TRACE 6A—UNITE 7A—BLIGHT
1D—NOTICE 2D—GRADUAL 3D—EVENING 4D—MOMENT
Double Bonus: Retaliate—AVENGE
Found in Europe—GENEVA

178. Answers:
1A—TAHITI 5A—VIRGO 6A—FLOUR 7A—CLIENT
1D—TAVERN 2D—HARMFUL 3D—TWOSOME 4D—PARROT
Double Bonus: Item—ARTICLE
A type of performance—RECITAL

179. Answers:
1A—GETUP 5A—CAPABLE 6A—PROFUSE
1D—GALA 2D—TUBA 3D—PILL 4D—CHAP 5D—ELSE
Double Bonus: Spirits—GHOULS
Swampy area—SLOUGH

180. Answers:
1A—ADDING 5A—ONSET 6A—ACORN 7A—CRISIS
1D—APOLLO 2D—DESPAIR 3D—NATIONS 4D—PLANTS
Double Bonus: Situated—LOCATED
This is something you can drink—COLD TEA